# Xiao Yu Dian: (Little Rain Drop)

# LITTLE RAIN DROP:

*Showers of Blessings from China*

Dr. Jeff Taylor

Order this book online at www.trafford.com
or email orders@trafford.com

Most Trafford titles are also available at major online book retailers.

Printed in the United States of America.

ISBN: 978-1-4269-3737-8 (sc)
ISBN: 978-1-4269-3738-5 (hc)
ISBN: 978-1-4269-3739-2 (e-book)

Library of Congress Control Number: 2010909430

*Our mission is to efficiently provide the world's finest, most comprehensive book publishing
service, enabling every author to experience success. To find out how to publish your book,
your way, and have it available worldwide, visit us online at www.trafford.com*

*Trafford rev. 7/21/2010*

 www.trafford.com

**North America & international**
toll-free: 1 888 232 4444 (USA & Canada)
phone: 250 383 6864 ♦ fax: 812 355 4082

*Dewey Decimal Classification Number:*
*Subject Heading: Adoption, Human Interest, Faith & Spirituality*

# DEDICATION

*To my precious little girl, Samantha, or "Xiao Yu Dian." That was the nick-name given to her in China, which means "little rain drop." Indeed, she is like the refreshing first rain of spring, showering us with a delightful blessing of laughter, love, and life. We knew from the start that someday, somewhere, she would want to know and understand the reasons why she was adopted from China. I hope that by this book she might see through the eyes of "my daddy," and that she will not only find her answers, but that she will know my heart. Daddy loves you "berry, berry much!"*

*To my wife, Debbie; we have shared extraordinary sights and experiences in our life together. We've seen the Alps, oceans, castles, Stonehenge, the Eiffel Tower, and many of the world's most magnificent sights and wonders. The greatest vision I've ever seen, however, is the glow of joy, contentment, and wonder as I've watched you hold our little girl. That sight stirs a warm and passionate place in the depth of my heart. Thank you for your love and friendship. There is no other person I would rather share life with: You are a wonderful wife and "mommy."*

# PREFACE

To know that you were chosen. To know that someone wanted you so much, they traveled half-way around the globe to find you and bring you home. To know that time, money, and red tape could not sway our deeply rooted desire to hold you. You were chosen.

What a profound concept: To be able to choose life. To make a determined, dynamic, and decisive commitment to rescue a child from abandonment and offer her a different future. An international adoption encompasses such choices; choices that impact the lives of a family and a waiting child forever. Given the wait, expense, complexities, and unknowns of adoption, not to mention the added intricacies of an international adoption, the journey itself can be a challenging experience. I can offer this encouragement: It is a choice that quickens the spirit and broadens your world beyond anything you may have previously experienced. It is a defining moment, brought about by a life changing choice for both adoptive parent and adopted child.

What a day and age to undertake such a pilgrimage. With the aid of the Internet, a digital camera, and digital video camera, we were able to share our experience in real time with our "team." I guess that is the best word to describe the numerous family members, friends, and professionals who would help us on this path. I have always believed it takes so many things coming together in perfect timing to develop a self-reliant and well adjusted being in our self-indulgent and dysfunctional world. What a difference it made to have our families, friends, and others standing with us, behind us, and rooting for us each step of the way. From the day we announced our intent, our parents, family, and friends embraced our decision to adopt internationally with open arms. We can never express the depth of our appreciation to Great Wall China Adoptions for their work both here and in China. As we set sail upon the voyage to bring our daughter home, we were truly blessed to have a great "team" in our corner. After all, the actual adoption is only the beginning of a far greater journey- parenthood!

When we first seriously entertained the notion of adopting from China, we were significantly impacted by meeting other families who had just done what we were about to do. We could relate to the desires that led them down the path of adoption. We were fascinated with their stories and drank in every detail about their journey. I'll admit that sometimes my ears stopped listening as my eyes watched the different little Chinese girls play, smile, sing, and frolic. It was at one such meeting that I started to envision the possibility of having one of our own. Dreams becoming reality. Little eyes looking into mine, a little head laying on my shoulder as I sing her to sleep, and a sweet little voice saying, "Daddy, I wuv ewe." Our hearts were quickly filled with a powerful resolve and determination.

From the outset, we decided to chronicle our adventure so that we might also share our story with those interested in adopting from China, as well as with family, friends, and anyone else interested. This home-made documentary is a collection of the proverbial "rhyme & reason" related to our choice to adopt from China.

Within these pages, I will answer the biggest question, "why." It is my hope that our story will inspire, encourage, and impact families considering this option. It is my hope that as she matures, my daughter will read these words and know "why." We have included photos, humor, and our own perspective in hopes you will see we are very ordinary people. Maybe you'll look at this and think: "You know, if they can do it so can we!"

One of my favorite poems is by Robert Frost, entitled *The Road Less Traveled.*[1] The poem has nothing to do with adoption per se; rather, it is about the choices we make in life. At first, the idea of traveling to China to adopt a child seemed as dark, ominous, and mysterious as the path he speaks of in his poem. One truth about taking a path that you've never been down before: It's a little intimidating! Too many unknowns, too many "what if's," and the inability to see what lies ahead on the path before you. It all starts with the first step. For us, it was a step of faith, a step I'll discuss in greater detail later. In the end, it was the path that made all the difference in our lives. We offer to take you down this path with us now, as we set out to capture our *Little Rain Drop.*

# Introduction

Adoption. It's such a common word. In today's society it's a common practice. Hundreds of children are adopted every day, tens of thousands each year. No big deal. Had I never embarked upon the journey of adopting my daughter, that word would be one of many within my dust covered dictionary. Of all the words I know, "adoption" is one.

Depending upon where you find yourself on life's "road less traveled," adoption is a word that can open a whole new world of wonder, and a word that can make a grown man cringe with fear. Before we'd ever reached a point in life where we were seriously thinking about a family, the word didn't mean much. When, however, the traditional and medical processes of biological conception failed, it was an idea that beckoned us closer. Once we were committed to this path, the adoption process became a dynamic, living, and breathing entity that took on a life of its own; an adventurous quest into the voyage of parenthood.

So, why document this journey specifically from a father's point of view? It's not that I feel compelled to create the "manly man's" version of our adoption story. This is merely one man's perspective as a father who went through the process of adopting a daughter from China. The tale within these pages is simply our story, or more to the point my story about us from my unique and sometimes warped point of view. Now, for those who were expecting the macho, tough dude approach, feel free to operate a power tool as you read along. I can admit that after twelve years of longing, my tears fell freely with profound joy when I held my little girl for the first time. Manliness aside, this tale is about the intense joy of becoming a father. There's nothing that can touch the heart of a man like hearing the word "daddy" from the voice of his little angel.

I decided to create my own little documentary for a number of reasons. For her part, my wife Debbie took the primary role of devoting herself to the mind-numbing task and countless hours of capturing the exhaustive paper trail, or "red tape." I believe it was former president Ronald Reagan who once said, *"Red tape is a lot like duct tape, but not nearly as useful and twice as sticky."* More diligent than Santa, she checked these documents once, then twice. Not a sliver of paperwork escaped her grasp. The end result is a sizable and impressive archive of more than a thousand pages of forms, lists, emails, official certificates, photos, and so forth. Her work is a chronology of our experience, and a road map that others have followed in their own adoption journey. She is my heroine, my love, and number one on my list of the "top 100" most admired women of the world. While she checked, rechecked, copied, authenticated, and labored over the paperwork, I decided for my part to record some of the more subjective issues, i.e., the who, what, when, where, how, and especially why.

As to my faith, this book is a "stone of remembrance." If you read the beginning of the Old Testament book of Joshua, the day Israel crossed the Jordan River into the Promised Land was a defining moment for both Joshua and the nation. For Joshua, it solidified him as the new leader of Israel following the death of Moses. For Israel, it was a new beginning in the land they'd been promised. Forty years of manna stopped flowing from heaven that day when they ate the produce of the Promised Land for the first time; a new day indeed. Crossing the Jordan, they carried the Ark of the Covenant out into the middle of the river. The waters receded and the people crossed over on dry land. Once across, one designate from each tribe was to go and retrieve a stone from the river bed at the feet of the priests who were bearing the Ark, and with the stones they would build a memorial in their camp. Joshua, in turn, took twelve stones from the other side and placed them in front of the Ark before the waters returned.

God commanded this action so that the people would remember this day, this defining moment in their history together, this new beginning. Listen to the reasoning: [These stones are] *to serve as a sign among you. In the future, when your children ask you, 'What do these stones mean?'*[7] *tell them that the flow of the Jordan was cut off before the ark of the covenant of the LORD. When it crossed the Jordan, the waters of the Jordan were cut off. These stones are to be a memorial to the people of Israel forever."* (Joshua 4:6-7, NIV). Throughout the Bible, people have marked defining moments with feasts, monuments, and "stones of remembrance." For my part, I felt responsible as Samantha's father to do the same.

Thus, this book is that "stone" for my daughter. I imagine that one day she will look at herself in the mirror and wonder about things. She already knows that she's different from her parents. She already knows that she was born in China, and she knows that she was adopted. Someday, however, she'll wonder "why?" She'll want answers about her past. She'll want to know about *where* she was born. She'll want to know about the woman who gave her life; about the mother who gave her away.

That is my objective: To answer the questions yet to be asked. She will deserve to know more than the "One Child Policy" that led her birth parents to abandon her. She will need to know the emotions, heart, history, and longing that led us down that road to her. She'll need to know something more specific about her circumstances, more about where she is from. I don't know if what I construct within these pages will satisfy her desire to know. All I do know is that I must be about collecting and cataloging the "why" for my little girl; creating a stone of remembrance for my daughter.

Finally, as seasoned international travelers, my wife and I knew this trip would be different from any of our prior overseas adventures. We've returned from London with teddy bears, from Germany with nutcrackers, and from France with perfume and cologne. This time, we'll return with a gift beyond measure. Our trip to China will not be about business, sightseeing, collecting souvenirs, or learning a new culture. It is a life-changing mission of purpose. A journey to connect two families, literally on opposite sides of the planet. A voyage to bring home our daughter. Such an undertaking in and of itself is filled with many things; emotion, courage, obstacles, and joy. I needed to record what we were thinking, feeling, and experiencing.

My hope is that you will enjoy this story as you share our experience. It is a story of love, a story of hope, and a look at God's providence. If you are someone who has picked up this book anticipating adopting a child from China, my prayers go with you. May God fill your heart with the joy of parenting, and may the bond that unites you with your waiting child be unbreakable. Peace for your journey.

# CHAPTER 1

## *The Saga Begins*

I'll never forget seeing the movie Star Wars®² for the first time in 1977. There on the big screen, the majestic overture trumpeted; "*Bommm - bommm, boppa ba bom bom*" as the now famous words scrolled upwards across the screen; "*Long ago in a Galaxy far away . . .* " (Feel free to listen to the original sound track as you read). That first impression trumpeted that a fantastic journey was ahead. For me, it is so much better than; "*Once upon a time, in a land far, far away . . .* " Nope; I'm more the Star Wars® kinda guy! It projects the feeling I get when I look back and remember the day that we made our decision: The day we said "*Let's do it.*" I knew then that we were about to set sail on a great adventure, so cue the music and hand me my light saber.

What transpired to get us to that point and what occurred afterwards in many ways seems a fairy tale. Never once in the twelve years prior to this experience did we remotely consider that one day we would literally travel to the other side of the planet, have a small, helpless little baby placed in our arms and return with her to our home. Even while we were planning the trip, it still seemed like some distant dream; A wisp of evaporating breath too frail to grasp and hold.

It wasn't until we were holding her in our arms that the dream gave way to reality, and the reality was a dream come true. We did, in fact go to a land far, far, away in search of a special treasure that awaited us there. We returned to a cheering crowd, and each day since has been our "happily

1

ever after." None-the-less, all stories have their starting point, so I'll start at the beginning. I hope that our story will create perspective as to our emotions and desires which led us to adopt. So, *"Long, long ago in a land far, far away . . ."*

In this first chapter, I'll tell you a little about us. By way of introduction, I am a man of faith. Ordained minister, seminary degree, the whole works. I've married and buried people by the hundreds. I've worked in a few churches, some full-time, some part-time. I believe in the Almighty with all I am. I haven't always worked in the church; My career goal was to be a military chaplain. Sometimes, however, life doesn't turn out the way you plan.

On May 17th, 1990, I entered my apartment to find my wife in a pool of blood. It was one of those life-altering moments that seem to make time stand still. Diagnosed as paranoid schizophrenic and severely depressed, she ended her life by her own hand. I discovered her a few hours later. I still have no words to describe the pain and devastation of that moment. In the years that followed, I realized that something had died within me. I struggled for years with post traumatic stress disorder. Emotionally, I knew there was damage, mostly expressed as apathy (blunt affect) about many things. Hands down, it was the most difficult experience I've ever faced.

Odd thing about the storms in life: The hits just kept on coming. After the death of my first wife and the end of the first Gulf war, bases were being closed and forces downsized. After meeting all the requirements, endorsements, and training as a US Army chaplain, I was shocked to find my career was essentially over before it began. After nine and a half years in the Army, I was out of a full-time job and had no intention to be a career reservist. As a widowed minister, I had another problem. Churches didn't want single ministers. My marriage ended, my career ended, I was very depressed. My only choice was to fall back on something else.

My other career is in Human Resource Management. Equally educated and trained for this field, I became an expert in employment and labor law, receiving the highest certification for HR Management, as well as a doctorate in the field. I guess either way you slice it, I'm in the people business. Even after I remarried, I chose to remain in this field for the next 15 years before returning to full-time church work. It proved to be a life changing choice.

By the time I reached my fortieth birthday, I had no complaints on the life I had lived thus far. Not that life has been easy. I have known heartbreak. I have known great joy. I have changed lives. I have made regrettable mistakes. For many years I didn't care if I ever had a child. Genuinely apathetic. If I became a father, fine. If not, just as well. Either way I was content; especially since I didn't know what I was missing. One great thing about getting older: Eventually, attitudes change.

My wife Debbie is one of the most extraordinary women I know. Throughout her life, she has been a solid, intelligent, and gifted young lady. She finds great pleasure in the simplest things. Her family is her life. By career, she is a seasoned Medical Technologist. If you think in terms of CSI, she is a "lab rat." Actually, she's a lot cuter, more like a lab hamster. But I digress. Debbie is faithful to be there day in and day out. Her character is impeccable. Her integrity is without reproach. Her loyalty and devotion as a wife redefined what I thought marriage could be. After what I had lost, I was beyond grateful for having her in my life. There is nothing I would not do for her. Ironically, the one thing she desired the most was something I could not give her. (See, the plot starts to thicken right away)!

**Jeff & Debbie Taylor, Dec. 21, 1992**

Debbie and I were married on December 21, 1991 in Fort Worth, Texas. We met in grad school and were married the day after I graduated from Seminary. From the time we started dating, we both felt the same about starting a family. Since this was my second marriage and due to our age (I was 30, Debbie wasn't), we didn't plan to delay having children. While we were engaged, we talked fondly of having a little girl, and frequently discussed potential names of our future child. Debbie is loving, nurturing, and tender. It takes very little imagination to envision Debbie reading a bedtime story with a little girl in her lap.

In the movie *Parenthood*[3], a young Keneau Reeves provides an interesting discourse about being a father. Comparatively, he observes that one needs a license to drive, a license to hunt, and even a license to catch a fish. Yet, any (expletive) can be a father. I get what he is saying. Good point, but not true. For most adults, becoming a parent is a fairly easy process. Sometimes it is planned, sometimes it isn't, and sometimes it seems a little more complicated. Sometimes, it takes the intervention of medical science. Sometimes it takes a miracle.

Now imagine that your greatest desire is to have a baby: To hold a precious little child in your arms. One of the strongest and most penetrating values of your character is a sense of family. Imagine the pain and agony that after years to trying, you are faced with the truth that you will never be able to conceive a child of your own. You look around at others your age, celebrating their children's birthdays, sporting events, and graduation, all the while aching inside with deprivation and a feeling of loss that you cannot experience these things yourself. Welcome to our world.

There is a story in the Old Testament of the Bible about a woman named Hannah. It's an astonishing story about a woman's desire for a child. She wanted only one thing in life; to be a mother. Hannah lives in a home where there are other wives and multiple children, but none of these belong to her. With the birth of each new child, Hannah feels more and more alone. Despite the fact her husband loved her more than his other wives and treated her like a queen, only one thing could ever satisfy her reason for being. For Hannah, being a mother *was* life.

In the first chapter of First Samuel, the emotions are raw, brutal, and intense. Following a worship service and dinner, Hannah gets up and goes for a walk outside. Her appetite is gone. With each step, the tears begin to trail down her cheeks and her knees begin to tremble. Her chest begins to quiver, her agony is profound. As she approaches the temple, the floodgates open with tormented bellows of grief. With deep and bitter sobs she falls down before God and pours out her heart with unintelligible words. Broken. Hurting. A wound that has never healed. She felt less than a woman, unworthy as a wife. The scene is painful to read; excruciating to think about.

As she lays there crying, her anguish was so great that she is perceived to be drunk by the priest. When I close my eyes, I can see her, hear her. The wailing that originates from the deepest recesses of the heart. To hear the sound would make you think the world would never know joy again. As she pleads her case, she vows to God that if He would but grant her a son, she would return the child to God's service.

Imagine such longing: *"Just allow me the joy of being a mother, and I will give back what You have given me."* In the end, God grants her request and she is faithful to her vow. She gives her son to Eli to be trained as a priest. In response to her faithfulness, she is given more children and her joy is complete.

My wife Debbie has never thrown herself before the altar of our church, but internally she was Hannah. That ancient story describes the desire and longing of her heart. I've seen the tears. I've felt the yearning desire of motherhood within her. With each passing year, hope slipped further and further away. I felt as if a part of my wife was dying.

By 1997, and after numerous procedures and doctors visits, the possibility that we would conceive a child of our own was about as hopeful as finding a bald gorilla in the wild. To cut to the chase: Not withstanding a miracle, neither of us could have children. Following this emotional devastation, we knew there was only one other option. It was at this point we considered adoption for the first time.

It's probably at this juncture I should disclose that the term adoption has many different facets. There is domestic and international adoption, closed & open adoption, special needs adoption, surrogate mothers, black market adoptions, and numerous con-artists. As we go further, I'll explain some of the above terms. It was overwhelming when we first considered it: That's why we didn't consider it for very long.

Our first shock was in reading about couples who had begun the process, shelled out tens of thousands of dollars, waded through the administrative and legal paperwork, and waited for the child to be born, only to have the biological mother exercise her legal right to rescind her decision within a few days after the child was born. I know couples personally who have been through such a nightmare. With "open" adoptions, there are no guarantees on how long you wait, if you will be selected, and whether or not the birth mother will follow through. There is likewise nothing the prospective parents can do about it, except play the game by the adoption agency's rules. We thought briefly about international adoption as we researched our options. In the end, the apprehension and uncertainly, not to mention the expense made adoption too risky for us. What to do? We couldn't have children of our own. We couldn't afford to adopt, and after what we'd learned, we really didn't want to adopt. What to do indeed.

We did have "substitute children." We've had Miniature Schnauzers since the first year we were married, and these warm, funny, and entertaining little characters filled the role for a while. Still, as much as we love our dogs, it's not the same. Besides, we soundly understood that the dogs would spend our retirement on squeaky toys.

We decided to distract ourselves by seeing the world. Sounds like a plan, doesn't it? Certainly: Visit ancient and historical places so that we could completely forget the aching desire of what we could not have. I wish I could look back and say, *"What were we thinking,"* but as it turned out, these adventures prepared us for a far greater journey.

Over the next five years, we were able to visit many other places and countries. At one point, we had even purchased a four by eight foot world map that we attached to foam board with map pins to designate our past, present, and future travels. Silly as it may sound, we genuinely thought such a thing could take our minds off what we really wanted. Honestly; what were we thinking?

In October of 2000, we managed to return to Huntsville, Texas, to be near Debbie's family after eight years in Memphis, Tennessee near my family. Due to the distance from Memphis, we had missed opportunities to attend family events in Huntsville like birthdays, graduations, and holidays. We valued these family events even more than ever, so we "loaded up the truck and moved to Beverly;" Huntsville, that is. With that move, my wife was able to meet her sister every week for lunch and enjoy various events with her family. We joined the same church, and even little events were a wonderful affirmation of family. We both had good jobs and life was good in general.

Of course, one small problem did tend to resurface from time to time. That's the funny thing about emotions. We would see a movie that had a baby related theme, or we would encounter others who had just had a child. Sometimes that would make us sad and remind us of one thing in life that we didn't have.

There were also times it seemed so unfair: Other's getting pregnant "by accident," abortion of more than one million babies each year while one million people waited on adoption lists (do the math). Then came the heart breaking stories of the absurd. We were especially angered over the grisly story of Melissa Drexler (and others like her): The degenerate teen who delivered her baby in the bathroom while attending her prom. She wrapped the helpless infant in plastic garbage bags, discarded her baby boy in the bathroom trash, then went out and danced at her prom while the baby suffocated to death. She was unremorseful, apathetic, repulsive. How could a woman do such a depraved thing? We felt like running a nation-wide article pleading with pregnant teens, "Don't kill your kid, let us have them!"

Considering how much we've been blessed with, it was never within us to complain about things we didn't have. Even so, we knew deep within this was still an issue. In life, you can only bury deeply rooted emotions so far before they resurface. Dreams die hard. The most profound desires of the heart live on.

# CHAPTER 2

## *Defining Moments*

Our history is in many respects similar to others who reach the decision to adopt. The details may be different and there are certainly other reasons to adopt a child. For most, I think adoption is a means to satisfy the greatest desires of the heart. There are defining moments in life, changes in the wind where circumstances align and the impossible becomes reality. Shattered dreams become a new vision. For a brief moment, a door opens and opportunity presents itself.

That defining moment came for us in 2002 during the weeks leading up to Thanksgiving. We received a call from Debbie's brother who came over to talk with us. Regrettably, his seventeen year old daughter had become pregnant. For some odd reason, he stated, *"She has decided to keep the child, and is not going to give it up for adoption."* He explained that they were aware how much we had wanted children, and expressed that his daughter did not want us to be upset with her for keeping the child. We weren't quite sure why he said this, but all the same, we were profoundly hurt. We felt as if we were somehow unworthy of being considered parents. We know there was no intent to offend, but it was a clear indication that our desires for family were still alive and unresolved.

Many of those deeply buried feelings started to come back to the surface. The feeling of unfairness had always been more distant, however, now it had hit closer to home. The pain, anguish, anger, and emotions became a sense of loss that was now on the forefront. After a few weeks, it became a bitter pill to swallow and for the first time in a long time, we started talking again about having a family. In fact, it became a daily topic of conversation. In time, we would have let it go; we always did before. As it happens, this was just the tip of the proverbial iceberg.

A couple of weeks later, Thanksgiving Day, 2002, we celebrated the holiday with Debbie's family in McKinney, Texas, (about an hour north of Dallas for those not from Texas). After the holiday meal, we enjoyed the traditional exchange of silly and entertaining "White Elephant" gifts. Honestly, we could have used a good laugh. Instead of the usual start to this event, however, Debbie's sister announced that her mother had to open the first gift. Her mother obliged: It was a pair of baby shoes with an announcement that Debbie's sister was pregnant. Everyone clapped, cheered, hugged, and celebrated. Everyone, that is, but us. Blindsided by the news, Debbie was stunned expressionless. I could see the hurt building on her face. Knowing what she was thinking, watching the expressions of pain and anguish surface, I began looking for an opportunity to get us out of there. We both just wanted to escape.

The conflicting emotions of trying to show some expression of happiness for her sister's news, while also attempting to cope with the deeply rooted hurt of our own inability to conceive was overwhelming. I'm not able to adequately explain the variety of emotions we were feeling at that moment, but it was the worst holiday we've ever celebrated together. From across the room, I could see the ache in Debbie's eyes. I knew her heart was breaking. I didn't know what to do about it.

We left the house that evening without saying a word. We climbed into my pickup to head to our hotel. We sat without speaking. All that I was feeling at that moment was being expressed in the deep sobs emanating from my wife. As we held one another, I could feel my own tears slowly gliding down my cheek.

That night, Debbie and I sat in my truck and talked, wept, and talked some more about what we were feeling. We were both on the same page: We still wanted a child of our own. As much as we had tried to suppress our feelings, the desire for a family resurfaced with a powerful vengeance. We also knew there was only one solution. That became a defining moment in our lives; the night we determined to adopt a child of our own.

We decided that we needed to go home and begin researching adoption again. We understood one thing above all else: Our desire for a family, a baby to hold, and the joys of parenthood were as strong as they had ever been. Perhaps the events of the past two weeks had finally helped us come to terms with our own hearts. Perhaps these circumstances were required to help us get to that place where we were emotionally ready.

We returned home on the Saturday after Thanksgiving and immediately started our quest. In the high tech, information overloaded world of the early twenty-first century, we found sufficient resources over the Internet which led to meetings, published literature, and a vast collection of materials about the subject. We started reading everything we could find about adoption; the good, the bad, and the ugly. We were shocked to read about those who steal babies and sell them on the black market, as well as con-artists that deceive couples desperate to adopt by pretending to be pregnant then skipping town as soon as they receive some money. Due to the expense and wait of domestic adoptions, it was clear how some couples could be taken in by the possibility of a quick and cheap alternative. At first, all the fears that were present before came surfacing up once again. Yet, this too helped us to think carefully about what we wanted and how we would accomplish our goal. It was clear from the beginning that we would need to work with a reputable agency.

We were very discouraged with the thought of an "open adoption." A "closed adoption" means that the records are sealed; no one but the court has access to information about the birth parents, and the birth parents have no knowledge of the adoptive parents, except for basic medical information. (Closed adoptions are now extremely rare). "Open adoption" essentially allows a birth mother to leaf through a book containing photographs and descriptions of prospective adopters and choose a couple she feels would give her baby the best home. She may never meet the adopters and this may be her only contact with them. Or, she may want ongoing contact with the child and adoptive family. The more we read about open adoption, the less we considered it.

Debbie started collecting information and diverse statistics concerning international adoption, including the costs and regulations related to different countries. We also found many conferences that would be held in the Houston area with various adoption agencies. These were information sessions that provided fee and cost structure, rules and regulations, and visits with families from that agency who had recently adopted abroad. The cost was about the same as a domestic adoption, however, the process and finality were more to our liking. We couldn't conceive of shelling out tens of thousands of dollars, laboring through the red tape, and years of dedication with the possibility at the very end a young mother could decide the day after she had the baby that she wanted to keep it. Although it doesn't happen that often, we didn't think we would endure something like that. The international route offered the options that appealed to us the most.

Additionally, international adoptions had increased dramatically since our last consideration in 1997, and the majority of domestic adoption agencies now offered international adoption services as well. Even in a small town like ours, we both knew people who had adopted a daughter from China. We had seen statistically that ninety-six percent of the children adopted from China were girls. We had settled on a girl's name very early in our marriage, and if one country could increase our chances of adopting a little girl, then that was the direction to go.

The more we met with different agencies and the more we looked at the assortment of options, the more comfortable we were with adopting from China. Pursuing the possibility of adoption consumed our holiday season so much so that we didn't even set up our Christmas tree. At Christmas dinner, however, we had made enough progress that we could announce to our families that we were going to adopt a little girl from China. The support for our decision was solid and never waned. The outlook for 2003 was getting brighter. Debbie and I had a renewed sense of meaning in our lives as we worked together to find our little girl and bring her home.

We reviewed web sites and information packets from agencies throughout the US, and attended a handful of adoption meetings during January and February of 2003. For those thinking about adoption, we highly recommend attending the information sessions set up by prospective agencies. You can obtain loads of information, you can ask very targeted and specific questions, and you typically get to meet with families like us who have recently returned with their adopted child. I enjoyed that the most, as these were the people who provided a genuine and candid disclosure of the process- without the "sales pitch."

We were most impressed with an agency called "Great Wall China Adoptions®" based in Austin, Texas; an agency that exclusively arranges adoptions with China. That is to say – they only handle adoptions from China; no other countries, no domestic adoptions. In addition to their corporate offices in Austin, Texas, they also have an office in Beijing, China near the Chinese Center for Adoption Affairs; (CCAA- the Chinese State agency that handles every adoption of a Chinese child). After listening to the stories of about a dozen people who had already adopted a child from China, knowing that GWCA has their own staff working in Beijing was very appealing. For instance, some agencies use third party tour guides for the international segment of the adoption. Some of the stories I've heard and read about were disheartening. Let's just say the third party types were less than motivated to watch out for us big nose Americans!

Looking back, we have no regrets with our choice. We submitted our application and initial fees on March 1st, 2003; the first tangible step in our commitment. We received notice about three weeks later that we were approved, and along with our acceptance we were given an "Adoption Journal" by GWCA to take us through the process: (This is the document that takes you through all of the "red tape" required for adoption, time lines, costs, and so forth). Thus, the paper trail had begun, or as some adoptive parents have phrased it, *"we were in our paper pregnancy."* Via email and the phone, we were able to ask as many questions as necessary to the Agency as we put together our "dossier;" the collection of papers and forms that would allow us to adopt. In short, the dossier is your entire life on paper, with verification and authentication of everything about you. The dossier is eventually translated into Mandarin Chinese. It's truly amazing to watch your entire life become summed up in a few dozen sheets of paper. Actually, I was not that impressed with my paperwork self.

As we started the paperwork, I began to contemplate "God's timing" to a greater degree. (This is what spiritual people do). As human, earthly beings, we live in linear time. We are born. We die. There are milestones along the way that we hold dear. God, however, is eternal. Everlasting to everlasting. He does not exist on a linear plane, although He does interact with it.

Why do I bring this up? It's the age old struggle of accepting or challenging one's station in life. First, we can't have our own children, so are we trying to circumvent God's plan for our lives? Perhaps that was His plan; who are we to argue? More on that in a second. The other issue is that there are quite a few warnings in the Bible about trying to make God's sense of time work within our sense of time. Trust me on this: You really want to wait on God's sense of time. You *never* want to try and force God's hand. Big mistake. Big no-no. And yet, how we try.

That very thing happened in the book of Genesis to a guy named Abraham. God spoke audibly (out loud) to Abraham and literally promised him a son; a bouncing baby bambino. Then God stopped talking about it. Many years had passed and nothing happened. Most of the people Abraham's age were now great-grandfathers. So, realizing they needed to help God out a bit, his wife (Sarah) handed over one of her handmaids to speed up the process. Long story short: *Abraham did get a son as promised, but not as planned.* God has His own sense of timing and God was not amused. In fact, the conflict that arose from that act of impatience is still in force today. The child born from Sarah's handmaid became the patriarch of the various Arabian nations. The child that was later born to Abraham and Sarah: The nation of Israel. Thousands of years later, they're still at each other's throat. The moral of this story: Don't try to force God's hand, (as if we could)!

Earlier in our marriage we could have forged ahead and adopted a child. There were opportunities, but there were conflicts as well. We never knew "peace," or a deep sense that it was right. We knew that other couples our age were becoming grandparents and their kids were graduating high school and college. The biological clock had stopped, but something within us was still ticking. All the same, we knew better than to try and force God's hand.

True to God's timing, now everything had aligned perfectly; (this is not a reference to the stars, just to our circumstances). It was beyond anything we could have designed. We were emotionally ready. We were financially ready. Many things were different, both with us and the process of international adoption. Through cash bonuses, stock options, and an adoption reimbursement, my job provided most of the cost for our adoption. We had support from everyone who knew us. Everything came together. Everything. We knew God's timing was at work.

It's amazing how fast the months can fly by. There was always something to do. About the same time we submitted our application, we purchased the house we were leasing and started fixing it up. We had numerous documents that had to be collected, certified, notarized, authenticated, and so forth. We were fingerprinted (twice), and had the most extensive physical exams either of us can remember in years. We moved forward diligently, one document at a time, making sure to do it right the first time. Actually, doing the paperwork is a good process: It gives you something tangible to do while waiting, which also gives you some sense of control.

Looking back, I've learned to appreciate the timing of different things. To give up on something that didn't seem right at the time, only to return later and find all is in order. The first week of August, we completed our paperwork and submitted it to the agency. Our agency would then send it to Beijing a few days later. Once the paper trail is complete, the true waiting begins. Another milestone reached, many more still ahead.

That same week, a woman in north-central China was approaching a defining moment of her own. She was preparing to do something unthinkable in my mind. She had reached the decision to give up her child; to abandon her baby that would eventually become our daughter. Perhaps it was the absence of something to do. Perhaps it was the sense of accomplishment in having sent off the dossier. Why it hit me so hard, I don't know, but it was all I could think of.

Someone we will never know sacrificed her rights to her own daughter. We would become the beneficiaries of her decision. From that point onward, I began to think about her from time to time. My heart was heavy for her. What right did we have to her baby? I felt like a transplant candidate waiting for someone to die so that I might have life. The conflict of emotion was alarming. I felt selfish. How could I be so selfish to benefit at the expense of a mother's heartbreak? Such choices. I will accept the blame, guilt, or any other dark emotion for this. This was her choice, her decision. Eventually, I took all I knew about her and re-created that decision in my mind; (it is the next to last chapter of this book).

After more than twelve years of marriage and when it comes to my wife, I can accept this scenario. I want to see my wife become a whole person. I want to fulfill her greatest desire. I remembered that Thanksgiving night in 2002, hearing her broken sobs as her body shook in my arms. I still feel her tears running down my neck. If someone, somewhere was willing for whatever reason to abandon her child, I will gladly do all within my power to find that child and make my wife a mother. That is my choice. I am willing to live with my choice.

Somewhere in Beijing, a folder that defines who we are was now in the hands of a Chinese national. I wonder what they think of us. Once they approve of us, the file will sit dormant until it is our turn to be matched with a child. The CCAA receives dossiers from various agencies throughout the world, sorts them into groups, and verifies that everything is intact. At the same time, the CCAA is sorting through files of children available for adoption throughout China, each one identified by a brown folder. Eventually, the thousands of families ahead of us would be "matched." That is the next major milestone in the process: What child will they match us with?

**The "matching room" in Beijing with files of families
waiting to be matched with a Chinese child.**

The letter was on ordinary, thin paper. The Mandarin script and official red seal made it stand out. On August 23, 2004, our dossier was approved, and we received an official notice from China in both Mandarin and English. I said to myself, "We're on the list." The waiting list. I don't know how long the list is, but we're on it. We have been officially recognized and accepted by the Chinese government to receive one of their abandoned children.

For obvious reasons, I began to hope that U. S. – China relations improve over the next year. I want them to like us. I want them to see us step off of the plane and say, *"We've been waiting for you: Welcome to China!"* Someday within the next year, an employee of the CCAA will pull our file and place it alongside the file of a waiting child. I hope they feel very good about that. I hope everyone in China involved with our adoption feels good about seeing a Chinese baby in our arms.

Now comes the hard part. As I mentioned earlier, while completing the paperwork there was always something to do. Now we just waited. To help pass the time, we busied ourselves with renovations to the thirty year old home we had purchased. We also found time to shop on occasion for things we would eventually need for the baby. We purchased a rocking chair for the room, then the crib. Tickets to Disney World. Started a savings account to pay for Harvard. A shotgun for her first date. Until we knew more about the baby, we stayed away from most clothing purchases, but found a few items we knew would universally work for a toddler.

First impressions are important. Our first meeting with our agency (GWCA) gave us the confidence that we could trust them fully with this important process. Process? Not quite the right word; how about "our life." It feels wonderful to see a first impression exceeded and our agency did exactly that: Exceeded our expectations on every level. For instance, our adoption agency sends each family constant updates by email; they were always in touch with us, even if there was nothing new to report.

There are multiple stages the dossiers go through: "*Translation*" where the file is translated into Mandarin; the "*Matching Room*" where prospective parents are matched with available children; and finally "*Referral*" where the agency and family are notified of the match. Throughout the waiting period, we received regular updates as to which stage we were in. Even if there was nothing going on at the time, we received regular emails to tell us that nothing had changed. When you're in the waiting stage, any news was good news: We were still in contact, we were still on the list. The constant communication affirmed that we had selected an agency that was very much in tune with the emotional stress involved in adoption.

I enjoy little surprises. Getting bumped up to first class is one of my favorites. A baker's dozen is pretty cool. You pay for a dozen donuts and there's one more. Debbie and I always appreciate when we receive a little something extra. It makes us feel special. We were feeling special as we saw 2003 come to a close. During the fall of 2003 and winter of 2004, many of the DTC (Dossier to China) groups were being doubled, (i.e., December and January DTC groups all had referrals), which meant the process was moving faster! Initially, we anticipated that we would be traveling to China around August or September of 2004. With two months of DTC groups traveling at the same time, we started to hope that we might travel even sooner. A shorter wait: That's very special!

As the spring progressed, so did our travel date. We knew our dossier was in the matching room at the end of January, and by the end of March, we knew that our referral was about to arrive any day. Our world was getting smaller; China was getting closer.

# CHAPTER 3

## *Distant Futures, Present Realities*

Defining moments. I watched Neil Armstrong walk on the moon-live. I was eight. I'll never forget it. I was in Memphis when Martin Luther King was shot. I was there when Elvis died; (the entire city was depressed). The events that impact our lives leave an indelible impression. The first time I saw her face, it was a defining moment.

On April 8th, 2004, the waiting came to an end. Debbie happened to be off that Thursday when the call came. We had received a series of emails over the past two weeks related to the activity at the CCAA, including a notice that our agency anticipated a new batch of referrals at any time. I think time stood still as Debbie answered the phone. GWCA called to tell us that we had received our referral. The case worker confirmed our email address and then forwarded the file. Within seconds, the email was opening.

Debbie was the first in our family to see *"Zhang Yu,"* (pronounced *Jong-You);* A nine month old baby girl born in Zhangye, China on July 8th, 2003. The email file included basic information about her along with four photos. She had been abandoned on August 7th, 2003, left at the entrance to the People's Hospital of Zhangye. She had been placed in a box, heavily clothed with a full bottle and extra milk powder. A nurse, (by the name of Shu Ming), was arriving for work and found the baby. She turned her over to the *Zhangye Social Welfare Institute* (the orphanage) where she would remain until adopted. Most importantly, we now lived in a new reality. Debbie called and squealed with excitement as she told me we had received our referral. Even though I was teaching a training class, I broke the group for lunch (1 hour and 15 minutes early), and "quickly" drove the four miles to our house. I wouldn't say that I was speeding, however, I did pass a number of others who were.

**Samantha at five months**

To say this was love at first sight would be a gross understatement. Her appearance was that of a happy, healthy, and beautiful little girl. I scanned through the four photos over and over again. Debbie had printed off the photos and taken them to show her parents and co-workers. Due to our then "dial up" internet connection, the final photo had not finished downloading before Debbie printed them. In that last photo, our little one was wearing a colorful little sun dress, holding a little doll, and had the sweetest little grin! That was the picture that stole my heart. I printed that one (an 8 X 10 no less), bought a frame for it and took it back to work to show my co-workers. For the rest of the day, I introduced colleagues and employees to my new daughter. I was already beginning to feel like a new dad.

Along with the photos were documents about her background, health, and disposition. We laughed at the comment on her temperament evaluation which asked *"What is her favorite toy?"* The response was *"all of them."* Zhang Yu was described in her growth report as *"active, having a ready smile, and laughs aloud."* The pictures agreed. If I could have turned cartwheels without destroying the furniture, I would have. We were absolutely blown away with excitement! Our immediate response was to email her photos to friends and family.

Consider the impact of this moment: After months of paperwork, then many more months of waiting, you finally have a face. This is her; this is the child we've been waiting for! Back in December of 2002, we had hope, prayer, and desire. Now, almost a year and a half later, we had a smiling little face looking back at us from half-way around the world. This is the little girl we'll be going to get in China. I now have a picture to carry in my wallet, a photo in a frame to keep on my desk, and a face to look at every morning and every night until I get to hold her.

Until now, the entire experience was mundane and abstract: Working toward adopting "someone." At this moment, you are confronted with object reality. It's no longer a dream and an endless period of waiting. She weighs so much, her hair is this long, she was born on that day. I absorbed every detail about this little girl over and over, trying to memorize and drink-in the details about her life thus far. For the next two months I had a continual lump of anticipation in my throat. I was really going to be a daddy.

Naturally, now that the target was confined to a specific area, we also wanted to know everything we could about her first home. Zhangye (pronounced *jong-yee*) is a small town in North Central China in the Gansu Province. This is a long, narrow province sandwiched between the mountains south of the Yellow River and the Gobi desert to the north. We would meet our daughter for the first time in Lanzhou, (pronounced

*Lon-joe),* the capital city of Gansu Province. We consulted our world atlas and immediately located the different towns. Although it would be another two months before we traveled, there was much to do.

For a guy who has taught time management and organization for a living, I cannot hold a candle to my wife's sensibility for detail. In preparation for this moment, Debbie had already purchased baby outfits, disposable cameras, and a small blanket. We slept with the blanket to infuse it with our presence. Debbie had the instructions translated into Mandarin, asking that Zhang Yu keep the blanket in her crib and that the orphanage keep the additional clothes and toys. With the cameras was attached a request to photograph routine activities of her day. We included a photograph of ourselves, also for the orphanage to keep. She then sent the package via Fed Ex to the orphanage.

**The Zhangye Social Welfare Institute (Samantha's Orphanage)**

No doubt, there was cause for celebration. On the day we received our referral, Debbie's parents invited their entire family to a local Chinese restaurant to celebrate the event. For many months we considered various names. I don't know if you've ever seen one of those "baby name" books: They have about a zillion names from every culture, to include what the name means. We had been through a few of those books numerous times and had picked a few possibilities. One name that settled well with us was

"*Samantha.*" After reviewing all of the potential names and looking over Zhang Yu's information, we made a final decision: We would name her "Samantha Claire Yu Taylor." At dinner that evening, we showed off the photos of our little girl and announced her new name. From that point on, everyone referred to her as "Samantha."

Now the real fun begins. Once you receive the referral, you are handed off to the "Travel Team." This is the department within the adoption agency that will actually make the travel arrangements. The date you depart is based on a number of things. First, after the emailed referral packet, we received the official hard copy of the documentation via Federal Express®. A form is inside which must be signed and returned with some urgency: A commitment to accept the child. You can take what time you need to review the medical history, social history, and so forth, however, the travel date can't be set until both parents have signed and returned the letter of acceptance. That letter is then sent to the CCAA and U.S. Consulate in Guangzhou, China. Once the U.S. Consulate is notified, they will set a date and time for the child and parents to appear for their appointment. This is the last official act of the process- at least while in China, and after the oath has been administered you get to go home! Thus, once that appointment is set for your group, the travel plans are scheduled so that all of the paperwork, visas, passports, and documentation related to the child can be completed before the U.S. Consulate appointment.

The travel team told us our Consulate appointment would be June 16th, 2003, at 1:00pm. In order to complete the process in China before that date, we would arrive in Beijing on June 4th, and we would receive Samantha on Sunday, June 6th. While we were pondering over this new information, we were also following other groups who would be traveling before us. We had met other couples adopting with GWCA back in April, some of whom would be traveling with us. The group that would be traveling before us would actually be getting their children on Mother's Day. I can only imagine what a wonderfully memorable event that would be for a first time mother: Becoming a mom on Mother's Day. Of course, in looking at the time frame scheduled for our trip, we would be returning with our daughter the Thursday before Father's Day; how perfect!

The travel team arranges all flights, tours, hotels, and transportation within China for the entire group; we simply pay the fees and leave it up to the Agency. It was our responsibility to make arrangements (which GWCA assisted with) for travel between Houston and China. While reviewing our options, and having made a few trips out of the country, we decided we would travel to China a few days early so that we could acclimate without being rushed. We wound up choosing flights that would have us entering and leaving China from the same place; Guangzhou (pronounced *"Gwong-joe."*)

There was also one last official bit of business to take care of as soon as possible. Once we had received our referral, we immediately went to the Chinese Consulate in Houston to get our visa to enter China. The visa is only good for ninety days, and you have the option of a single or multiple entry visa. Of course, this is critical: Without the visa, you don't get into the country. In fact, without the visa, you don't even get on the plane. The process requires that you leave your passport and documentation with the Chinese consulate (along with a fee), and they return your passport to you about two weeks later with the visa adhered inside. I'd never allowed my passport out of my sight before, so this was a little un-nerving. I was very happy to see that Fed Ex® package arrive the following week!

I also did one other thing the week after receiving our referral. Based on many other trips out of the country where foreign currency was involved, I've always found it helpful to order some of the currency ahead of time so that when you land and need to eat, get a taxi, and so forth, you'll have enough of the local currency on hand to get you by for a few days. For example; since the original plan had us arriving in Beijing on a Friday, a conservative estimate tells me that I'll either have to attempt exchanging currency in the airport (at the worst rates and long lines), with the hotel (depends), or on Monday at a local bank, provided it's not a holiday. It's a good idea to research the country and its currency laws. Most major US banks can order foreign currency for you with a week's notice. As it turned out, this process has always allowed us to collect our luggage, eat, and move immediately to a taxi stand without having to worry about whether or not the taxi driver would accept dollars, and without standing in a long line attempting to exchange money at the airport after a long flight. Yup, just a little tip there for 'ya from the travel guru!

# Chapter 4

## *We Must Away*

There's something about the shimmering and streamlined bodies of aircraft that fascinates me. I stand watching them land, move, and power down the runway. Despite many years of business travel, my inner child still comes alive in an airport. I love to travel. I am filled with expectancy for the journey.

In a word, "anticipation" can describe our hearts and minds as we departed to finalize our adoption of Samantha. I stood at the window studying the steel and aluminum fortress that will speed us towards our destination. My foremost thought is "*Wow, what a journey!*" It is amazing to finally arrive at this point. One week from today, we will meet our little one face to face. We will hold her next to us. We will be in awe and wonder. We will make baby noises that will confuse and baffle our Chinese hosts. We will be proud parents. We are on our way.

It was a phrase we've heard in a number of British comedies. A peculiar line that has stuck with us for more than a decade: "*I must away.*" We use it at different times for different reasons; most frequently when leaving the house to go to work. Oddly, those words have crossed my lips at least twice today. Debbie is alive in a way I've never known. She laughs when I say, "*We must away!*" Our private joke. Underneath her cool demeanor beats a racing heart. More than for myself, I have done this for her. Despite the fact I could spend 24/7 on an airplane, Debbie does not share my fascination. We will land in China about 24 hours from now and Debbie will not sleep a wink. She doesn't sleep on airplanes. She will be exhausted when we reach our final destination. I have prepared. She will be fine. It is my plan to make this part of our lives memorable. Let the plan unfold. *We must away!*

We were transported to the airport by Debbie's parents and we have plenty of time to relax. No rush. We have checked, double checked, and confirmed. We have everything with us. With passports, tickets, and carry-on bags in hand, I push Debbie forward as they call for the First Class passengers. She has never flown first class. The look in her eyes says everything. It is a treat to pamper my child's mother. It is important to begin our trip well.

It will take four hours to reach Los Angeles on the Delta 767. She grins when her meal is served on real china. In Los Angeles, we will transfer to comparable business class seats on China Southern Airlines for the fifteen hour flight to Guangzhou. I think this will be the last American food we'll see for a while. I am wearing my travel watch with two faces. On the left, one face keeps the time at home: On the right, the time in China. My child is soundly asleep right now, preparing to wake and begin her day. While in country, we will be 13 hours ahead. It's all happening too fast; one more week and she'll be ours.

Around midnight "Houston time," we transferred to our overseas flight at LAX. The bulkhead was in front of our seats. For my six-foot, two inch frame, that means another foot of leg room in seats that recline almost horizontal. I am a happy camper. The Chinese attendants are demure and polite as they serve dinner. I have three woks at home. I love Chinese food and prepare it often. I have a wide palette. I am willing to try most anything. What they served us in-flight, however, was from the Twilight Zone. It appears to be a combination of things from the sea; things that should have remained in the sea. We hope that this unidentifiable food is not a sign of things to come. I will be so disappointed.

As the lumbering jet liner strains to its final cruising altitude, I have changed into lounge wear. I have put on my compression socks (feet swell when flying at high altitudes for extended periods of time). I can sleep at the drop of a hat, ball cap, small visor, etc., so the flight will be uneventful for me. After a good 10 hour snooze, I may be able to recall something of the trans-pacific flight; I doubt it. The multiple jet engines should effectively drown out my snoring. To help Debbie pass the long hours while I doze loudly, I gave her my laptop. I've brought along some of her favorite

DVD's to watch and games to play to pass the time. I am fighting the "Z" monster: I am losing the battle.

As I drifted off to sleep, I went over and over in my mind the hasty job of packing. Did I forget anything important? Since everything I own is made in China, I figured I could replace it fairly easy. For my part, I had two duties. I would be the pack mule. While Debbie carried the munchkin around, I would carry the diaper bag, food, and the cameras. Diaper bag - check. Bottles and burp tarp – check. Cameras - check and check. The other role of the adoptive father is to be the AV Guru. We are the chosen ones who document the event with thousands of digital photos and an endless loop of video tape. We are expert cinematographers. We will edit, slice, add sound and special effects. I'm certain my home adoption movies will be all the rage at the next Cannes Film Festival.

The anticipation of what lies ahead is weighty. For the last six weeks, her image has been on our minds. I hope she has that precocious smile waiting for us that we've memorized from her photo. Her name is on our tongue, and in a few days, we will meet her face to face for the first time. My heart races and my head spins the more I think of that moment.

We will distract ourselves until that moment with getting acclimated to China, shopping, and mastering the Chinese language in five days; (well, two out of three anyway). Yet, in the back of our minds will be this little baby we are longing to hold. We don't know what she'll think of us, and I'm sure she has no concept of what is about to happen to her. I hope she is accepting of us, and that the shock isn't too much for her. If she can sense the deep and powerful love we feel for her already, she'll know that all is well in her world and the bonding process will be underway. Tonight, just like every night for the past two months, I will dream of our child. I don't know who wrote the original, but I beg they'll forgive me as I re-write this prayer:

*Now I lay me down to sleep,*
*Our path is set, our child to meet.*
*Keep her safe, secure, and warm,*
*Until we come to take her home.*
*Amen.*

# CHAPTER 5

## *The Other Side of the World*

In cartoons, you can dig straight down through the earth. In a few minutes you pop out upside-down in China. I can tell you that in reality, it's a much longer journey. I've never spent that much time on an airplane for a single flight. I think we'll just stay and buy a house here; I don't want to fly back to the US for at least a few years.

Our flight was without incident and the service was astonishing. Our flight attendants were courteous, polite, and very attentive, frequently bowing and checking to see if we required anything further. We were provided with a sleep mask, slippers, and a toiletry kit to freshen up at the end of the flight. Next thing I knew, it was time to get up and eat breakfast. Prior to this trip, I thought I knew a lot about Asian cuisine. I was wrong. I would try to explain the food we had for dinner and breakfast, however, I'm just thankful at this point that I've kept it down. The unidentifiable elements had an equally inexplicable flavor, texture and color: Nothing I'd want to keep for my culinary journal.

Debbie has been awake for about thirty hours; she is exhausted. As we will be arriving at our hotel in the early morning (six AM China time), I pre-arranged an early check-in time with the hotel. I couldn't think of her having to sit in the lobby of a hotel for six hours until the official check-in time. She will take a warm shower and collapse on the bed. She should be up and around in a month or so. We are staying in a five star hotel with a well deserved reputation for service. It is a beautiful place, and the room and amenities are very nice. Each floor has an attendant to press the button to the elevator as soon as they hear someone emerging from a room; thus, the elevator is waiting on you, not the other way around. More about these wonderful attendants later.

We landed at the Guangzhou International Airport and Sauna around five-fifteen, right on schedule. After being "glared" at for about a minute by the customs agent, we went into the third world baggage claim (the chickens weren't awake yet) where we lost about three pounds from the surreal heat, humidity, and total absence of ventilation. When I say, "absence of ventilation," let's forget about the luxury of air conditioning: There was no air movement whatsoever. Perhaps they don't turn the AC on until the temperature reaches the three digit figures in the building, or the tourists falling out from heat exhaustion reach the double digits. As stifling as it was at five-thirty in the morning, I can hardly wait to come back in a couple of weeks when we land at noon: It should resemble Dante's Inferno by then.

I can't express the sense of relief you feel when you are half-way around the world and you see your luggage arrive on the carousel: All is well. Queue Handel's Hallelujah Chorus. We've never lost luggage on a trip before, but we know folks who have. We also figured out that the baggage handlers here must get paid based upon the amount of damage they inflict upon the luggage. Our guy was well into the bonus money. We understand the airport is due for its annual cleaning in about five months.

During our travels in the U.S. and abroad, Debbie and I have been on some interesting taxi rides, and this one was definitely in the top ten. We had the "lean" going on pretty well: That's when you know you're about to get hit, so you lean the opposite way. Oh yeah- we did a whole lot of leaning while riding with our Nascar® driver-in-training. It was also amazing to see the traffic for six in the morning. It kind of reminded me of Houston for a minute. Well, except for the bicycles loaded with vegetables, and the motorcycles loaded with vegetables, and the three wheeled trucks loaded with vegetables . . . you get the idea.

We were even behind one truck that had an open air cage in the back with about two dozen sides of beef & hogs hanging there, rocking back and forth, being attacked by flies and who knows what else. I made a note to avoid that particular restaurant. The mass of vegetables on each vehicle was at least ten times the mass of the vehicle itself. Beans, cabbage, fruit, and so on. If you go to your favorite produce department and it's empty, you'll know where all the vegetables went. I also saw various people out and about beginning their day. Street sweepers with huge brooms dressed in yellow jump suits, shop keepers washing or sweeping the sidewalk in front of their store and so forth. I'm awestruck at how busy this place is so early in the morning.

We arrived at the hotel just after six in the morning, and after unpacking I took a wonderful hot shower, after which I wrapped myself in a bath towel the size of a twin bed blanket- literally! I try to be quiet, but at this point Debbie could sleep underneath a roaring jet engine. While she rests, I'll be headed down to the business center to send an email to family. For our first day, we planned to have a quiet schedule of rest and relaxation to get over the jet lag. I'll run my usual travel errands. Priorities: Diet coke, snacks, cash some traveler's checks. Yup; that's enough for one day.

So what is it with "the glare?" I went down and around the corner to the *Bank of China* to cash in some traveler's checks. The dude at the bank, the policeman on the corner, the customs agent: They all look at me with "the glare:" This evil, penetrating look that makes you want to confess to hiding Jimmy Hoffa's body. I think everyone in uniform has x-ray vision: They stare as if they can see right through me. I'd never felt like a criminal until I entered the bank that morning. Within seconds, I was sure I was on China's top-ten list of known felons. Every eye was on me. These were not friendly eyes. I feel guilty; please tell me what I'm doing wrong.

I'll say one thing about the work ethic here - it is very high and very serious. The young man who took my traveler's checks examined them against my passport very thoroughly- again, and again, and again (while he glared at me). I assume this was his idea of professionalism. I think the use of both an adding machine and a calculator was overkill, but hey- he wanted to do a good job! For fear of getting shot, I'm trying not to glare back. After he handed me my money and passport, I felt like asking permission to leave. I'm ready to go back to my hotel please.

After a brief six hour nap, Debbie is awake. It's time to explore our surroundings. For lunch today, we headed to a local favorite of American tourists in the park near the hotel, "Lucy's." We had a hamburger (no veggies) and fries, with a diet coke, or should I say "Coke Light." I've seen pictures of a coke machine when soft drinks were a nickel; late 1950's I'd say. Never thought I'd pay that little for a can of soda, but that's about what it costs here. Simply amazing.

Next to our hotel is the *Shamian Park*. At one o'clock in the afternoon, there were people practicing a festival dance routine, ball room dancing, Tai Chi, and playing a variety of games. The Chinese people here are very active, friendly, courteous, and from what we've seen in the first hour, tend to fill their time with meeting people, being active, and socializing when not at work. Not a bad way to spend an afternoon wherever you live. It is a splendid culture mixed with deep tradition and cutting edge contemporary technology.

The park and area surrounding the hotel are also filled with bronze and stone sculptures. One of the contemporary sculptures in particular grabbed my attention. The sculpture was of three women from three different ages. One from 1800 in the ancient and traditional dress, one from 1900 in the outfit of a poor laborer, and the final young woman representing the year 2000 in short-shorts, a polo shirt, sun glasses, and a cell phone pressed against her ear. What a statement about how times change.

For dinner our first night in country, we ate Chinese food, which makes sense . . . because we're in China. To be fair, one cannot simply say, "Chinese food" to describe Chinese cuisine any more than one could say "American Food." Our country is diverse: Seafood specialties of the east coast, southern cooking, Texas BBQ, and of course the whole west coast thing. China is much the same. Here in the southern end of China, the predominant style is "Cantonese." The menus here in town are very interesting: If it moves, flies, swims, or stands still long enough, it is on the menu and we have photos to prove it.

For instance, try "*boiled snake with orange zest*," or "*oil fried pigeon with sea cucumbers*." Come to think of it, no wonder we didn't see any pigeons in the park today. Turtles, bats, insects: The offerings of food here are as bizarre as they are undiscriminating. I ordered a diced chicken and noodle dish for Debbie, and I had Peking Duck (of course). Since Peking is now Beijing, I wonder if it should be called Beijing Duck? I also loaded my back-pack before we left the states with dozens of plastic forks for Debbie: She doesn't do chop sticks. I'm just happy I didn't have to explain the dozens of plastic forks while going through customs.

Throughout the first floor of the White Swan Hotel is a collection of jade carvings worth thousands of dollars, such as a seven foot tall Chinese junk and a very intricate pagoda. There were many beautiful items to see in the stores on the first floor, including hand carved elephant tusks (which are illegal to import back into the US). Someone has been very naughty.

Overall, we are very impressed with the White Swan Hotel; it is everything a five-star hotel should be. Before I forget, let me get back to the floor attendants: A hostess on each floor around the clock. If you need anything, she will get it for you. Even if you don't know you need it, she will still get it for you. For example, when we returned from dinner our first night, there was a crib in our room. I guess if they see an American couple here not in business attire, they assume we are adopting; (this hotel handles more than seven thousand adoptive families a year, more than 200 while we were there). We politely explained the crib was a couple of weeks premature, and they politely removed it. The floor attendant seemed a bit dismayed; almost insulted that we didn't want the crib. I'll leave her a tip; I think $10 (a week's salary) should do. Our beds were turned down for the night, chocolates and fresh bottles of water were left behind, and we were indeed ready to turn in. We were told the beds were fairly hard by the GWCA travel team, but we didn't find that to be the case, just properly firm. Certainly didn't deter us from our earlier nap, and I doubt we will have any trouble sleeping. I'll need my rest: Tomorrow I'm attending a seminar on "The Art of Glaring Back."

# Chapter 6

## *Culture Shock*

The card said it all. Some pictures truly are worth more than a thousand words. The card left an image I can't get out of my mind: A large, brown grizzly bear holding a baby panda. Yup, that's about to be me. The words inside wished us well on our journey. It was given to me the day before leaving Texas by a man who has been where I now walk. Along with the card was a gift for our daughter: A plush doll named "Ling." The man who came to my house was my pastor; His daughter is Hannah. She was born in China. They have made this journey. From the very beginning, this family has shared our experience. They have re-lived their experience through us; they are for us, they are with us. We are so very much aware of the love, prayers, and support from so many family and friends. We'll spend the rest of our lives saying thank you!

All in all, we've seen about five to six dozen American families with their little Chinese babies tooling around the hotel and surrounding shops during our first few days in China. So many babies in snugglies, strollers, and various contraptions, it is clear why they've nicknamed the White Swan the *"Stork Hotel."* For those that don't know, a snuggly is a harness type device that allows the baby to comfortably hang from the mother's shoulders either facing the mother, or facing away. Position the little tyke facing forward, the child can assume control and steer the parent wherever they wish to go; a clear favorite of the little ones, flapping their little arms and legs in excitement as mommies shopped. In the face to face position, the device provides the little feet unrestricted access to the ribs and other vulnerable parts, as well as quick access to the parental steering device known as hair.

Guangzhou is the final destination for adoption before returning home, as the U.S. consulate is about one block over from the hotel. It has been great to talk with those just completing the process and hearing about some of their details. Everyone loves to talk about what they've done over the past week, things that have helped them and so forth. One curious thing though: I've met six mothers today who all named their daughters "Anna." I guess that's the name of the year. It also makes it hard to wait, just seeing so many people with their precious little ones. Sunday will be our turn; this is really happening.

We spent most of our first week in China window shopping, imagining Samantha in different outfits, enjoying each other's company, and thinking about friends, family, and our three "furry" children back home in the kennel. We start to laugh, then to worry. Our dogs are not the best behaved. Sparky has been renamed "Barky" by most of the staff; he just can't shut up. They'll probably never let Cozette, Sparky, and Sheba stay in that kennel again.

A word about "squeaky shoes." Sitting in a restaurant of a five-star hotel, one does not expect to hear one, two, then dozens of little "squeaks" surrounding him. It was like a pack of baby sea gulls learning to attack a helpless little fish en mass. Before my trip to China, I had never heard of such a thing, but my wife had. Squeaky shoes have little devices in the heel that squeak, thus teaching a child to step heel then toe as opposed to walking on the balls of their feet. At first, it is entertaining to hear many little feet squeaking around the floor while waiting for the elevator. Then a devious thought crossed my mind. How about squeaky shoes for all the little ones back home! I'd be banned from family events I think.

During our second night at the hotel, our floor hostess struck again. This time she gave us a Barbie holding a Chinese baby - the *"Going Home Barbie."* It is a traditional gift from the hotel for all the American families adopting children. I'm wondering if she is curious as to why she never sees us with a baby. I wonder if business men, new to working in China, scratch their head in bewilderment when they walk into their room and find a crib and a Barbie doll. I'm sure it makes a great story to share when they get back home.

One of our favorite things thus far is the best international breakfast buffet ever - it rivals Sunday brunch at the Summit Club in Memphis or the Petroleum Club in Houston. The buffet presents Asian, European, and

American (Western) foods, so everyone can find something to their liking. A chef prepared my omelet to order as I waited this morning; I am spoiled already. Yes, let's go ahead and move here. I'm sure I could find a house within walking distance of this breakfast buffet.

In our preparations for the trip, we read quite a bit about the cost of living in China. In the country, those in rural areas might earn about $500 a year. We read about doctors in rural towns that earn around $200 a month. Everything else is provided by the government. In cities like this, pay is more diverse. Foxconn, who employs more than 800,000 people, pay college graduates anywhere from $1,200 to $3,000 a year tops, as well as a bunk in the dormitory, meals, and full medical in the company health & welfare clinic. Believe it or not, the chance for that kind of money brings in hundreds of applicants a day from all over China. It is hard to believe everything is so inexpensive. Tonight, we went all out; really splurged on dinner. We had chicken fried rice, ginger chicken with scallions, and 2 diet cokes. Two dollars including the tip. I'm going to enjoy my stay here; tomorrow I'm going house hunting.

As we draw closer to meeting our daughter, we are having fun watching the babies pass by in strollers. Apparently, they aren't used to having things on their feet. Every child, (and I do mean "every"), were all trying to get their shoes off. Tugging, pulling, yanking, kicking. It was very funny to watch. I think most of them have never worn shoes, and it was equally obvious that their new American parents had been doing a lot of shopping for their new little babies. Cute outfits for everyone. Well, almost everyone. One poor child was wearing one of those *"what were you thinking"* outfits that no child should ever be forced to wear. Not sure what the style was intended to be, but it resembled long johns that had endured a tragic washing machine accident. I'd guess right about now the little girl is asking herself, *"who are these people, and what did they do with my clothes?"*

Ten years ago, everyone would have had to wait until we returned home to see the three of us together as a family. Now, we can send out an email with photos and video at the end of our day, or upload them to a web site, and folks back home get to see it at the beginning of their day. Adoption in real time: An awesome concept.

And yet, all is not wonderful in the Land of Oz. The pollution in Guangzhou is so bad it blocks out the sun. There is a gray haze here every day, which combined with the humidity makes the air feel heavy, thick, and slimy. Of course, that gives us an excuse to take another shower. Back to the towels again; I've never seen towels that large. Maybe I should check with the floor hostess to make sure we're not drying off with spare blankets. In addition to the air pollution, the water has issues as well. We are using bottled water for almost everything. The water in China contains varied levels of bacteria, pollution, and "non nutrients" that will ensure "Montezuma's Revenge" for all who are not acclimated to the consuming the local water.

Speaking of water, I enjoyed reading an email of a family that traveled a month before us. The mother was so paranoid about the water, that she brought a roll of duct tape to cover mouth, nose & ears while showering. The father thought it was a bit "over the top" and didn't use it, however, made the comment that if you see a photo of a twelve year-old American girl with no lips - that was his daughter. We left our duct tape at home.

At least 200% humidity (well, that's what it feels like). All you have to do is walk outside the air conditioned hotel and you can feel the breath being sucked out of you. Spending too much time outside means a change of sweat soaked clothes. I carry two bottles of water whenever we leave the hotel and buy more as we need it.

I also discovered a spice and food market about a mile north of the hotel. My discovery led me to the following revelation: There are simply things on this earth that were not meant to be consumed by humans. What I've witnessed thus far takes me back to a high school insect collection. I've stepped on the things that I've seen skewered on kabobs. How about scorpions on a stick. Locust, bugs, beetles, and little critters that don't look familiar . . . nor appetizing . . . on a stick. Other things were available for consumption that I have killed out in the yard at one time or another. Bats, flying lizards, snakes, rats, frogs, and the list goes on and on. We even saw a dog that was being butchered. Not only was the carcass of the dog being prepared for cooking, all of the entrails, the head, and the feet were also being processed for consumption. They boil the head & feet to create a soup broth. The entrails are grilled, minced with herbs and then stuffed into sausage casing. The dog was being prepared for a wedding: I'll remember that the next time I cater a wedding and see what the couple thinks about that as an option. I'm sure the locals were wondering why this crazy American was taking pictures of the food. We had been warned not to try the foods of the street vendors: Now we understand why- no concept of what the mystery meat might be.

Just when I couldn't look at any more "food," we happened upon an "American" restaurant, or so we thought. Pizza Hut®. We could hardly wait to dive into a pizza. Cheese, pepperoni, veggies. Enough weird food on a stick; let's have something normal. Then we saw the menu. Interesting options for topping a pizza that I, in my foolish and limited palette had never considered worthy to be pizza toppings. How could one not enjoy a slice of trout pizza? Or for that matter, a pan pizza with turtle- (as in the hard shell, four legged turtle– not the caramel & nuts "turtle"). For the gourmets out there, consider a thin and crispy pizza with lamb kabobs and peanut sauce, or the "Pigeon Supreme." I've been so deprived until now. What say we go with plain cheese.

Chinese history goes back so much further than ours. More than five thousand years. The Chinese invented the noodle. I'm wondering, however, who invented the squat toilet? This is a porcelain hole in the floor with two foot rests on each side. No seat, so you have to have fairly good balance. I wonder what people with one leg do? The water flushes below the opening, so after a couple of hours, the smell is, well- ever been to an outhouse in the middle of August??? There you go! Needless to say, we had the "western" toilets staked out, or else you had to hold it until you get back to the hotels.

# CHAPTER 7

## *The Big Nose View of China*

Sight-seeing wasn't the primary focus of our agenda in China, but we were able to do a little. The primary tourist event: The Tour of Death! (Every time I say that, I hear ominous music in my head- *doom, doom, doom*). The day before we are to get our daughter, we are scheduled to tour sights in or near Beijing all day. More on this later: First- more about the Guangzhou Airport.

We returned to the Guangzhou Airport in preparation to meet the rest of our group in Beijing. Upon entering through the main doors, the first thing that hits you is the smell of rotting leche nuts which are sold everywhere. Downstairs, upstairs, and everywhere else, there is no getting away from them. The locals eat them by the fist-full then toss the seeds and husks in the garbage, which judging by the odor is emptied only once a month. The stench was very tough on the stomach. I think it even permeated the time-space continuum.

Second, the Guangzhou airport has about 200 chairs for 3,000 bodies, which meant a three hour wait for us with nowhere to sit. We managed to sit on our luggage for about an hour before a couple of seats opened up. Just about the time we got to sit down, our gate opened and we had to move on.

The tour will occur on June 5th, 2004, the 15th anniversary of the 1989 massacre that ended the student uprising. While in the hotel at Guangzhou on June 3rd, we were watching the BBC edition of CNN. During the broadcast, a reporter was at Tiananmen Square talking about the changes from the uprising fifteen years ago. She stated the government touts sweeping change and reforms during that time, and then made the comment, *"But there are still many who do not agree."* That was the last we saw, as the station went blank. All the other stations were available, but this one was censored. About ten minutes later, CNN was back on the air. I guess the Chinese government is still a wee bit sensitive about the killing of those student demonstrators. Our guides mentioned that there may be protests tomorrow, and that we should not photograph, talk, or have anything to do with anyone protesting. These things made for a profound reminder that we were definitely in a country with limited freedoms. It made me wonder what else we might see concerning the constraint of liberty and intolerance. I suddenly realized how very far away from home I really felt. Let's get our baby and head home!

The day before we meet our child, we were scheduled to visit Tiananmen Square, the Forbidden City, and the Great Wall of China. After breakfast at the hotel, we boarded our bus and made the half hour drive into downtown Beijing. It is truly amazing the amount of bamboo scaffolding in use around some very large buildings. In the states, we're used to seeing the typical steel scaffolding with large planks to walk on. In Beijing, these are solid bamboo poles tied together with twine that rise ten stories or more. Amazingly, it is extremely sturdy, and is the same process that has been used for thousands of years to build things in China- so why mess with it if it works???

As Beijing prepares for the 2008 Olympic Games, the city is already undergoing a facelift. Overall, what we saw looks like most any other major city, except of course that everything was written in Mandarin Chinese. We did not see much of the capital other than traveling into and back out of the city. As the second largest city in China, some 13 million people, one thing that stood out was the massive number of high rise apartment buildings. These are typically called "matchbox" apartments, due to their small size- roughly about 600 square feet or less. They tower sixty stories into the sky here, there, and everywhere. I wonder how many of them have the luxury of an elevator?

Tiananmen Square was our first stop. All morning long we were surrounded by street merchants hawking their stuff. They had kites, maps, souvenir books, and so forth, and boy oh boy did we stand out! It was like a group of vultures swooping down upon their prey. The most interesting were the little guys with these cheesy plastic watches that featured a picture of Chairman Mao on the face. They would walk around with a dozen or so in each hand saying, "Rolex, Rolex." I pointed to my watch and said, "Timex, Timex." They were not amused.

The square (which is surrounded with government buildings and museums), is a place where a million people can congregate quite easily: It is the largest public square in the world. We walked through the square as our guides identified the different buildings. As we came to the street that separates the square from the Forbidden City, the entire group gathered for a photograph. Behind us was the entrance to the Forbidden City that sports the ten foot tall photo of Chairman Mao. In the photo, Mao's picture is directly above my head.

**Our adoption group in front of the Forbidden City**

The Forbidden City was built in 1406, and housed the royal families of 24 Chinese Emperors for more than 600 years, with the last emperor being ousted just before WWII. There is an Academy Award winning film called "*The Last Emperor*," which is, of course, about the Last Emperor of China who died in 1967. The first half and last few minutes give very good views of what this place looks like. The entire complex houses over 900 buildings and is the epitome of Chinese architecture. I don't remember how many hundreds of acres this thing is, but it looks bigger than the University of Tennessee. We walked straight through the middle of the complex; it took three hours. Yes, I'm talking a very large place! Our guide was also very happy to point out a "Four Star Toilet" near the end of the tour. This is a western style toilet (which means it looks like what we would have in our home). In China, such a thing is a luxury. We all took pictures of the "Four Star Toilet" sign. We're such tourists.

It is called the Forbidden City, because the emperors were seen as gods and the general public was not allowed access to them. Our guides told us that the place has only been open to the public for about 30 years, and many of the older Chinese people will not go inside for fear of incurring the wrath of the spirits of the previous emperors. I think if they can eat the bugs & creepy crawlies I've seen, they've already incurred some kind of wrath.

We headed north into the mountains, but first stopped for lunch as a group. I should say something about our adoption group as it will shed perspective on events. Our group is comprised of thirteen families, including us. Four of the families had been through this process before, and three of the families brought the children they had previously adopted with them. Three of the families had nannies, friends, or parents with them. Therefore, before even getting our babies, we have twenty-nine adults (including the two guides), and three children between the ages of three and five. That means that we always travel by means of a large passenger bus, and going to dinner together was a huge undertaking! Once you add in the babies, that will be forty-five beings on the bus. So, going to lunch and dinner today was a very impressive enterprise. We had to entrust ourselves to our guides and let them order the food for us, as the menus were in Mandarin.

We had ample opportunity to walk off lunch when we arrived at a section of *The Great Wall of China*. I say section, because this thing is spread out over about ten thousand miles, and not entirely pieced together. It was started in 770BC, and continued being built until the eighteenth century (Ming Dynasty), roughly off and on for two thousand years. Let me tell you one thing for certain: It would never pass building codes in the United States. The steps to this thing range from a few inches to over a foot in height, and it is incredibly uneven. I made it about half way to the first tower before my left knee started throbbing and swelling from an injury suffered a month earlier. Debbie continued up to the tower and took some nice photos. I've suggested that with the walking in Tiananmen Square, the Forbidden City, and now the Great Wall constitutes a tactic by our adoption agency to make us so tired that we would be able to sleep without the anxiety of what tomorrow holds. If that is part of the thinking, I can tell you it doesn't work: We were now tired and anxious! Thus my calling today, "The Tour of Death," because we're dead tired.

After returning to our hotel, we walked a little ways to a very nice Chinese restaurant where our national guide ordered dinner for all of us. We sampled fourteen amazing dishes, got filled to the gills, and for two people I paid a total of six dollars. This was also a very exclusive restaurant, and that price included a two dollar tip. Back home, that would have only covered two glasses of iced tea.

Cindy also wanted us to try what she claimed was a "moderately spicy" national dish; "*nothing too extreme*" were her exact words. When the dish landed, the flowers on the table began to wilt. For starters, there were more peppers than chicken. Now, living in Texas and having a fairly good tolerance to spicy Mexican food, I figured I was going to be fine as long as I only ate the chicken and didn't get a piece of pepper. I picked up my chopsticks, made sure there wasn't a single speck of red pepper on the chicken, and sampled it. After spending the next half hour drinking from a fire hose, I decided I'd had enough of the volcano chicken. At the end of the meal, our guide and waitress noted that the plate of "burn a hole through your stomach chicken" was still very full. I'm sure Cindy thought we were all wimps. If this is moderately spicy, I'd hate to see what she calls "extremely spicy." I'd probably just burst into flames once the dish got within ten feet of me.

Our stay in Beijing was only one day. If we ever come back, we'd like to see more of Beijing and the surrounding area, including the world famous Beijing Opera, (which has nothing to do with what most think of as Opera- it is dance and choreographed Kung Fu in elaborate make up and costume).

One final note about our one day in Beijing: China has managed to send its first astronaut into space this year on an orbit around the earth. While preparing for bed and watching the BBC's edition of CNN, they translated as the astronaut expressed his grave disappointment: You cannot see the Great Wall of China from outer space.

# CHAPTER 9

## *"Gottcha Day"*

The adoption agencies and parents who have been here before call it *"Gottcha Day."* That defining moment in life where you hold your child for the first time, that first face to face encounter. For the past couple of years, we've been looking forward to this day. For decades to follow, we'll look back upon this day with fond memories.

The better part of Gottcha Day was focused upon traveling to the city where we would meet our daughter. Unable to sleep the night before in anticipation of the milestone events of this day, we were up and packed at four in the morning. Our flight to the north-central city of Lanzhou would take about three hours from Beijing, followed by another hour on a bus from the airport to the city.

We arrived at our hotel about four o'clock that afternoon, and were told to be at the conference room on the twenty-second floor at 4:30pm to get our babies. Of course, all thirteen families dumped luggage in their rooms and went immediately up to the twenty-second floor. This was the moment we had been waiting for. At approximately five minutes after four, everyone was standing in the hallway outside the conference room.

There were three different orphanages in this province bringing children to the capital city. When we arrived upstairs, two of the orphanages had already entered the conference room, so we all peeked in the door to see the nannies and babies. At exactly four-thirty, those in charge started calling families in to get their children. As they started calling the names, our orphanage from Zhangye, China arrived and came down the hallway

41

towards the conference room. Samantha was the third baby in the line, and we recognized her immediately. Debbie bounced and squealed with excitement, *"There she is!!!"* As Samantha's nanny carried her past us, Samantha looked at us and smiled. Actually, it was more of a smirk, (which I now know is her default expression). She was within a couple of feet, and we stood in stunned excitement as she went by. Though I can't say with certainty what was going through the mind of this baby, she looked at me as if to say, *"What up, dude?"* All the same, we couldn't escape the realization that we'd just seen her: She's real, she's here. In just a few moments, she'll be in our arms.

After she had passed, I stood in the doorway of the conference room. The nanny was now seated with Samantha in her lap. I waved to get the nanny's attention, then pointed to Samantha, then back to me, trying to communicate, "She's ours." Understanding my impromptu sign language, the nanny turned Samantha towards me, pointed, and said to her, *"Ba Ba, Ba Ba,"* which is Chinese for "father." She then held up Samantha's right hand and started waving to me. Unimpressed, Samantha continued looking everywhere else other than at me. It's no wonder: She's probably never encountered a male, especially not one from America. Even if she could understand, I doubt at that point "Ba Ba" would have any meaning.

My heart leapt into my throat when I heard my last name called from inside the conference room. *"Taylor!"* With video camera running, I followed Debbie into the room where the nanny was holding Samantha. Debbie was carrying the required paperwork to hand over to the officials. Despite the understanding that I would fulfill the role of AV Guru, I was far too anxious to see what was going on. This resulted in some interesting footage of my feet, the ceiling, and many other wonderfully useless shots. Regaining my composure during the excitement, I focused the camera to record this monumental event in our lives.

Debbie showed the officials our passports and documents, and with no additional fanfare, they handed Samantha to her. Samantha went to Debbie with a pleasant but curious expression. They connected immediately, and Samantha couldn't stop looking at Debbie; she was transfixed. As we touched, kissed, and held her, the deep sense of joy and awe were overwhelming. She was really ours! We're really holding this baby. We soaked in every detail about her. Her smile, the grunts she made to communicate, the wet diaper. She was so tiny, so little, but the moment in time was so very large. It seemed that for all we were taking in, Samantha was also studying Debbie very carefully. She looked at every aspect of Debbie's face, and more than once put her hand on Debbie's cheeks, chin, and mouth.

**Debbie holds Samantha for the first time**

Samantha spent the rest of the evening clinging to Debbie, always staring at her with that curious expression. We took Samantha down to our hotel room. As beautiful as she was, Samantha didn't have that new baby smell. We changed her wet diaper and clothes and cleaned her up. This did not make a good initial impression on her. She started to cry, and then she started to scream. Okay; nothing wrong with the lungs- check. We hurriedly cleaned and redressed her lest the Chinese version of Child Protective Services thought we were torturing the poor thing. As soon as Debbie picked her up again, the tears and screaming stopped and all was right in the world again. We packed up the diaper bag and met our group downstairs. Now continues the paperwork and process.

Actually, we were both so physically, emotionally, and mentally exhausted, it's hard to describe our feelings at all. I still have the biggest lump in my throat and such a full heart after she wrapped her tiny little hand around my finger and smiled at me! I melted, I'm wrapped, I'm a daddy. It's almost too much to take in; I hope the feeling never wears off.

As for a description of our daughter, she has very short, thin-brown hair, and a ready smile. She grunts a lot in an effort to communicate, and is fascinated by things that make sound. Samantha is eleven months old, however, developmentally she is closer to five or six months. She has no teeth, she cannot crawl or even sit up by herself, and is still predominantly bottle fed. We try sitting her up, but she falls over and cannot remain in a seated position. Her fine and gross motor skills are also significantly underdeveloped. She doesn't close her hand around anything we give her, be it a toy, a puff treat, or even her bottle, but she does like to touch everything – exploring with her hands. It is clear to us that the babies have not been allowed to use their hands, and her every movement is filled with uncertainty. When in the snuggly, she does use her left hand to grab one of the straps; however that is the only time she closes her fingers around something. We were aware that this would be the case by the various professionals and other parents who have adopted from China, as well as their assurance that once exposed to the appropriate stimuli, the children catch up quickly. For us, it's an additional blessing. We knew the child we would get would be close to a year old. Yet, with the delays that we've encountered, for this moment in time we get to enjoy a little baby! We thought she'd be bigger and further along. We weren't really expecting this, but holding a little girl and feeding her a bottle gives us a small additional piece of the parenthood puzzle. She truly is our "baby" girl!

We got back to the hotel about 7pm, and were told that one parent from each family needed to go back to the conference room and start on some of the paperwork with the orphanage directors. Since Debbie completed the bulk of the documentation, she went and I stayed with Samantha, charged with getting her ready for bed. It's been a very long day for Samantha too, and the poor thing cried horribly when Debbie left the room. They said on the bus they only needed one of the parents for thirty minutes, which turned into two hours. If I could have, I would have called the conference room to see what's up. I need to consult my language guide to see how to say "Whazzzzuuppp!" in Mandarin. As I watched Samantha finally go to sleep, I wanted to shout at the top of my lungs, "WE GOT HER, SHE'S OURS!" I don't think she'd appreciate that one hour into her sleep, so maybe someone back home can take care of that for me.

# CHAPTER 10

## *Getting Acquainted*

The nanny told us that Samantha has a nick-name: In Chinese it is "*Xiao Yu Dian*," which means "*little rain drop*." Our guide wrote it down for us in Chinese and English, which we gave to a street artist to create calligraphy scroll. The nanny, the orphanage director, and both our guides kept calling her this, which makes Samantha giggle and wiggle about whenever she hears it. Learning about Samantha was such a joy and I wish we could have spent the rest of the evening just playing with her. That Sunday night, "Gottcha Day," was one of those defining moments meant to be savored and enjoyed. Unfortunately, there were a few hiccups to accompany our defining moment.

When Debbie went upstairs to the meeting, this is where Sunday went really down-hill. It was about 7:00pm, and we had been up since 4:00am. Neither of us had eaten since about 11:00am on the flight in, and we were already exhausted both physically and emotionally. They said the meeting would take about thirty minutes: Two hours later, Debbie had still not returned.

When Debbie left the room, I checked Samantha's diaper which was wet, so decided to change her and get her ready for bed. That's when the crying and screaming started, which I expected given the first diaper change. What I didn't expect was for the crying and screaming to last nearly an hour before she finally passed out. I rocked her, walked with her, sang to her, laid her in the crib, on the bed, gave her every toy we had, and finally offered her tuition to medical school if she'd stop crying.

She didn't want a bottle, wouldn't play with her toys, and continually cried "*mama.*" She didn't want me to touch her, jerked away from me, screamed louder when I picked her up, and kept looking around the room calling out for mama when I picked her up anyway. I knew this was a part of the process: She is now apart from everything familiar and I think the fear of the unknown had finally hit her. Poor thing; physically exhausted, in a strange place with a strange person who doesn't sound or look like anyone she's ever seen before: Deep voice, hairy lip, funny smelling American guy. I was kinda scared myself, and for the first time in a long time I felt absolutely helpless. In fact, I was also in unfamiliar surroundings with people I couldn't understand, hungry, tired, sleepy, and exhausted. So, I joined her, and we both cried for about 10 minutes. We rocked back & forth together for a long while. I then laid her on my chest and started singing lullabies to her until somewhere after the 8th song she finally fell asleep. Mental Note #2: Go immediately to holding her against my chest and singing when she won't stop crying. I laid her in the crib, and covered her with a baby blanket. I think we were both ready for the day to end.

From that point on, Samantha had a good night: I wish I could say the same for us, but it's like Murphy's Law: "*Things often get worse before they get better.*" That is precisely what happened. At 8:30pm, and Samantha now sound asleep, I ordered room service and made a brief journal entry, and at 9:00pm, both the food and Debbie got to the room. Debbie was about to fall over, as was I. We ate about half the food, being careful to remove the lettuce and tomato from our club sandwiches, and then I went down to the business center to send a quick email while Debbie got ready for bed.

When I returned and collapsed on the bed, Debbie and Samantha were asleep. About 10:30, however, our night ended as we started suffering the effects of food poisoning. Debbie threw up twice, and I had similar issues. Now that I think about it, I don't believe the mayonnaise was supposed to look like that. Throughout the night, we made many trips to the bathroom, and by 5am, we were beyond tired. I can't describe how horribly drained we had become, which was now amplified by illness and a severe lack of sleep. Not that we had anything important to do Monday; oh, like say adopt a child in a foreign country? We held each other a little while and then prayed together for God's strength. Despite how miserable we now felt, our thoughts turned to our baby. As the sun rose, we were on our knees offering her to God and asked His guidance in raising her. We spent the rest of the early hours talking. We were so worn out that we could not sleep. Fortunately, our problems did not keep Samantha from sleeping soundly for nine hours.

# CHAPTER 11

## *Becoming Daddy*

I don't know who invented Pepto Bismol®, but they are now our new best friends. Being seasoned international travelers, we've come prepared. We started taking the medications we brought with us, and the Pepto seemed to help quite a bit. We had some watermelon, fruit juice, toast and hot tea for breakfast, even though we had no appetite. Samantha had her bottle then really enjoyed a form of rice porridge called "congee." We dressed her in a cute little ladybug outfit, a little hat, and off we all went at 8:00am to the government officials who would finalize the adoption.

Samantha was bright, cheerful, and grinning at everyone we met. We were not any of those things. Running on empty, we were very fortunate to be the first couple called. At 9:00am, we signed the paperwork, passport application, birth certificate, and so forth. We paid our fees then put our thumb prints and Samantha's right foot print on the documents. This made it official: According to the Chinese government, Samantha was now ours. Hot diggity dog! (That's Texan for "wow").

The nanny who had carried Samantha from Zhangye to Lanzhou and handed her off to us was also there. She went around hugging the babies, holding some and carrying on with them all morning. This made us a bit nervous, as we didn't know how Samantha would react to seeing her again. Not in a very good mood and feeling horrible, I grabbed the first available weapon and prepared to smack the nanny with a wet wipe. Amazingly, when the nanny reached out her arms and clapped her hands inviting Samantha to come to her, she only smiled and held on tight to Debbie;

she would not go to the nanny! It was clear the bonding had begun, so I holstered the attack wet wipe for another time. We gave Samantha a small bottle of water, after which she slept for two hours. When the morning ended, all the families, babies, and orphanage staff took a group photo, then the nanny said goodbye to each baby she had escorted. As the director and Samantha's nanny left to start their long journey back to Zhangye, the nanny wept softly as she left the room; it was clear to see how much she cared for these children. She had also given us the disposable cameras that Debbie sent two months earlier. We did this in hopes of seeing the orphanage, as we will not be able to go visit during our stay.

Once we had finished the paperwork, we started to relax. All the formality was done, so for the rest of the week we can get to know this bundle of joy. We go in on Friday to collect the passport then fly to Guangzhou on Saturday to apply for her US visa. We were all going shopping for strollers, more formula, diet coke, and other such things, which the guides mercifully put off until 4pm. After lunch, we gave Samantha a bottle then put her down for a nap. We joined her and all slept for about two hours. We went shopping, bought a stroller, bottled water, formula, and diet coke, and then walked the 10 minutes back to the hotel. Samantha doesn't care for the stroller yet. In fact, Debbie has called her the "velcro baby." She has been in the snugglie most of the day when we've been out, (Samantha loves the snugglie). She clings to Debbie like a little monkey and has a fit whenever she's not with her. When I hold her, change her, or whatever, she throws a fit. When she gets back into Debbie's arms, she stops crying and looks at me with a grin! Actually, it's more like a little smirk, as if to say "You gave in sucker!!!" But I'm not worried- Just wait until she wants her own car. Samantha would not let anyone else hold her all day, and whenever Debbie had to do something and I had to hold her, Samantha immediately went into her tantrum mode.

After dinner, we returned to our room to rest. Samantha gets fussy when she's tired, rubs her eyes, yawns, and fights going to sleep. As she lay in her crib having a tantrum, (Debbie was getting ready for bed), I lay down across the bed, looked down at her and did the only thing I knew to do: I started singing. During the first 24 hours, that had been the most positive part of my relationship with this tiny little child: Singing her to sleep. Otherwise, she only tolerated me as long as Debbie was around. So, I started singing the first thing that popped into my mind- a song called "*Somewhere Out There.*©4" It just seemed so fitting at the time, so I sang to her very softly.

As soon as I started singing to her, the most amazing thing happened: She instantly stopped crying and stared into my eyes. With each little hand grabbing her blanket up under her chin, she gazed at me almost without blinking as I kept singing, never taking her eyes off of me. She had connected with Debbie almost instantly but was never very sure about me. So while I sang to her, a bond evolved over those few minutes that wasn't there before. That's all I can say to describe it- we really connected; just the two of us. Those little eyes fixed on mine, and she just kept staring and staring. As a proud father, I freely admit that the tears began to roll down my cheeks and my voice started to quiver as I sang to her until I could only hum; the words were lost. The most peaceful look covered her face as she drifted off to sleep, and my heart was full to over-flowing. It was a very special moment in time that I don't think I will ever forget. I sat there for about five minutes just watching her sleep, letting the tears fall, then kneeled down beside her crib to thank God for her. I don't really know if I had gotten through to her or if the connection was real: All I know is that she now had my whole heart. I lay down on the bed beside my daughter, enjoying one of the most peaceful night's sleep I'd ever had.

# CHAPTER 12

## *Bonding with Baby, Becoming a Daddy*

During our week long stay in Lanzhou, we decided to spend most of our time hanging out at the hotel to bond with Samantha. Due to the obvious developmental delays, we thought our time would be best spent helping her work on some of her gross and fine motor skills. Debbie started with her on her stomach, which initially led to something of a tantrum and tears. Throughout the week, however, Samantha worked diligently, pushing up and holding herself up with her arms, as well as starting to get her knees under her. Samantha worked hard each day with grins and a lot of energy, showing us some remarkable determination to get up and crawl. That was a great sign, and I was filled with wonder at what each day would hold. She also started learning how to actually grip and hold toys and snacks, and by the end of the week could pick up and put down objects. We had complete confidence that she would catch up very quickly!

Of course, Samantha wasn't the only one in need of training: Being a new daddy comes with certain challenges as well. I'd tried to ready myself in the two months prior to our trip, but now was the real deal. How do you get ready to handle a baby? Research, research, and more research. My research told me that a baby's body is capable of transforming common foods into a toxic biohazard, rendering the disposable diaper into a lethal weapon of mass destruction. I knew I had to be prepared- lives were at stake. Well, a little practice helps too, but unfortunately, I didn't have anyone willing to loan me their infant for a day. Probably for good reason given my plan of "Strategic Military Baby Tactics." Having spent nine and a half years in the US Army, I was used to training for dangerous situations in preparation for the "real thing." So, I approached the duties of fatherhood with military proficiency. I also learned a new non-verbal communication from my wife which involved her rolling her eyes in disbelief.

The most intimidating thing in my mind: Diaper changes. Absolutely no experience in this area and I was terrified but determined. While in the Army, I learned many useful things. I was a dangerously skilled warrior. I've been trained to operate more than a dozen weapons, I can kill with my bare hands, and can neutralize a target a mile away with morning breath. As the top graduate in my boot camp training brigade, I received awards and medals for my fierce and tenacious leadership. During OCS, I single-handedly ambushed and annihilated two enemy platoons. My enemies fear me. Brownie scouts salute me. I laughed throughout the Rambo movies. I am an expert marksman, I can make explosives out of toothpaste, napalm out of peanut butter, and I've jumped out of perfectly good airplanes. But when I encountered my first full diaper, I started searching for a white flag of surrender, begging for mercy before passing out. While stationed abroad, I was always prepared for biohazard warfare: Oh where, oh where was my gas mask now! I should have made a stop at my local military surplus store before the trip.

Yet, that is the purpose of an intensive military training regimen: To belay fear and attack the problem. Once I regained my composure, I went right into my "precision diaper drill." I had purchased two things to help me with this apprehensive task. First, I had picked up a half-dozen boxes of deodorizing, biodegradable plastic trash bags which were specifically designed to help contain the diaper to be disposed. As my wife shopped for baby bottles and bibs, that was what caught my well trained military eye. Only six boxes? How long would it take to get a case? Do they come in camo? Realistically, how would you like to be stuck on a bus for an hour-long ride to the airport with a toxic diaper? Exactly my point. Or how about a fifteen hour flight back to the US? Something like that could bring down the whole plane. Before leaving, I triple bagged my armory of disposable diaper sacks and filled the pockets of the diaper bag and my back pack.

The other consideration was keeping the diaper on the baby. Our only statistics were from a full medical at age five months. She was now eleven months, six months bigger. Since we couldn't bring a bag of diapers in each size, we would need to make adjustments on the fly as we didn't know what kind of diapers they had in China. The solution came to me while shopping in a local hardware store. On the paint aisle was a rack filled with nearly a hundred different types of tape. Some for painting, some for packaging, some for holding the pick-up truck together another thousand miles. Then I saw the old stand-by: Duct tape. Oh, but not just the standard dull gray duct tape, this place had colored duct tape! Black, orange, pink, camouflage. Could it be? Yes, white duct tape! I knew immediately I'd found it: The universal diaper repair and adjustment medium. If one of those impossible little tabs broke or ripped off, instant repair. If the diapers in China were too big, I could run a strip of duct tape around the legs and waist for a fashionable little belt. I was so proud, so prepared. Of course, looking back, all of the disposable diapers in the US said "made in China." Duh. Didn't think of that.

I also prepared in advance for one of my other new daddy duties: Burping the baby after the meal. My research included talking with other new fathers who had incredible war stories to tell, some suffering with post traumatic newborn disorder (nervous ticks and panic attacks when the baby cries). It seems we males are readily associated with the elimination of bodily gases for some reason. The trick, I was told, is to move the baby a moderate amount to reach optimum gas release. Too little, and the baby would experience discomfort with un-expelled gas, resulting in lengthy crying sessions. Too much, and the burper becomes the target of projectile vomiting by the burpee.

Courtesy of a pre-trip baby shower, I was introduced to my first "burp cloth." My immediate response: *"No, no, no, no, no. I have socks bigger than this thing."* Back to the paint department; there it is- a drop cloth. Yup, just a small opening for the head and we're in business. It was large enough to cover all the vital areas, allowed the arms unrestricted access to holding and burping and was completely washable. If the baby barfed, I would have enough canvas to move her to a dry spot for the post burping snooze. It was at this point of my strategic military baby tactics that I realized what Debbie's new expression meant: Something akin to *"you're an idiot; step away from the baby."*

This has nothing to do with Samantha, but it was really weird so I have to say something about it. During our stay in Lanzhou, we took a daily walk to a local park to get some fresh air. On the way there one morning, we saw what we thought was a street vendor getting arrested. This guy was arguing with five uniformed officers; (perhaps the first indication that he was making a HUGE mistake), who then responded by knocking stuff off of his cart. When they'd had enough arguing, one whipped out a small club and took the guy down in two hits, one behind each thigh. Two officers grabbed his arms and kept smacking him in the back of the head as they drug him off, another officer took his cart and the last two officers followed behind. We stayed out of the way, and tried to act like we hadn't seen anything. (I didn't want to be glared at again). When I told our guide about this later, she said the man was not being arrested. She said if the vendor didn't have a permit or littered, these "code enforcement officers" would require him to pay a fine immediately. If he didn't have the money to pay the fine or argued with them, they would take him immediately to the court to be sentenced, and they would probably take his cart if he didn't have the money to pay. Okay; if that's the fine for loitering, I'd hate to see what a "real" arrest looks like.

When we got to the fountain near the middle of the park, we made the mistake of stopping in one place for too long. Americans are very rare in this part of China, and once you stand in one place more than two minutes, you tend to draw a crowd. Not to mention the sight of two big nose Americans holding a little Chinese baby. So, before you know it, we have about two dozen people standing around us, all reaching in to touch Samantha, and all reading our cards about why we are in China. The locals are very friendly and never pushy or rude. On this occasion, I happened to back away and get a photo. We also had a student journalist from the University of Lanzhou stop us and two other couples on the way back to the hotel and ask about our adoptions. He said he wanted to write an article for one of his classes, so we talked to him for about five minutes.

Most evenings, our guides took our whole group to a very nice restaurant for dinner. There are usually eight to ten people with babies at each table, and each table has about four servers who wait on us hand and foot. As you can imagine, it takes a coordinated effort to get all of us in one area for dinner, but they have consistently managed to do just that. Cindy, our national guide, typically orders for us as the menus are all Mandarin. We will have a dozen dishes, plus an egg custard for the babies (which they all had in the orphanage and love), not to mention the smallest dinner plates in existence. She does a great job at getting a marvelous variety of food, and everyone always walks away satisfied and in awe of some of the Chinese dishes we've never seen or tasted before.

We're all exceptionally happy that our national guide, Cindy, doesn't order any of the more "exotic" dishes. Some dishes are much like the Chinese food we have in the states, and some are very different (which I can't wait to prepare at home). Then there's the price; a fairly high end restaurant, including drinks cost 60 yuan, which is about $7 US for the three of us. These dinners as a group are also the place that Samantha really comes alive. She loves to eat, tries to grab everything on the table, and when the egg custard comes out, she flaps her arms, opens her eyes really wide and chatters like a little chipmunk.

*"We have come here from America. We come to your area to adopt a new daughter.*
*We will love her very much, give her wonderful*
*growing environment, and a happy life."*

Apparently, Samantha was a bit of a favorite at the orphanage. Our guide, Cindy, has also developed a solid bond with Samantha, and passed on a request from the orphanage director to mail some photos of Samantha over the next year. Cindy asked if we might email a couple of the photos on occasion to her as well. Cindy has been married for eight years and lives in a small village in Southern China. Her mother wants to talk of nothing else other than why there are no grand-babies yet. She said if she could find another baby like Samantha, she would adopt her and take her home. For some reason, we decided to hold Samantha a little tighter.

Another baby from the Samantha's orphanage is named Rachael. Each night Samantha and Rachael sat together at dinner and it was very clear they knew each other. We videotaped some of their interaction. They reach out for one another and smile at each other. Rachael is not like Samantha; she is typically very quiet. When her parents saw the reaction, they were amazed as Rachael began chattering, laughing, smiling, and flapping her arms when Samantha came close to her. One thing all six babies from Zhangye share in common is blowing raspberries! They do it a lot and then giggle about it. None of the other babies do this, but all the Zhangye babies do. Beware one and all: This may be how Samantha says "hello." Bring a hanky to wipe your face afterwards.

Debbie reminded me to mention the journey to the restaurant our last night in Lanzhou. On some ventures, we take a large bus. Sometimes we walk, which we did that night. In front of our hotel was the main drag through Lanzhou; a six lane highway with a large tree filled median in the middle and a never ending flow of vehicles. To get to the restaurant, we had to cross this street without the help of traffic signals in a country where driving apparently involves seeing how close you can come to something without actually hitting it. When I say "traffic," it includes motor vehicles of all types plus about a million bicycles. The cyclists are everywhere and tend to weave in and out between the pedestrians. Traffic signals mean about as much as the dirt on the ground and it's a wonder there isn't a wreck every five minutes. So, crossing a large highway like this was a bit scary, but when an opening in the traffic started to emerge, our fearless and tenacious Cindy marched out into the street and held up her hand then waved us across. Not sure if the traffic was going to agree with Cindy, we were all a bit hesitant, but started cautiously into the street anyway. Sure enough, the cars stopped, honked, but stayed at bay while Cindy held up her hand and exchanged words with a couple of the irritated drivers. As soon as the last stroller had passed, the vehicles all started turning sharply to go around us. Disclaimer time: Please do not try this at home without a tenacious Chinese guide!

That morning (Friday), we took a trip down to the Yellow River to see a massive water wheel (still in use), as well as rafts made from inflated sheep skins. Some of the members in our group were bold enough to actually get on the inflated sheep skin rafts and float around in the river: I was wise enough to stay on the bank and take pictures. Afterwards, we stopped at a monument by the river where a group of women were practicing a dance for the Moon Festival. This followed by lunch at the "Noodle" restaurant: Not really sure of the name, our guides simply called it "the noodle restaurant." This area is known for its regional specialty, - you guessed it - noodles. We enjoyed the food and taped the demonstration of how the noodles are made. I don't think that Samantha had ever seen a noodle before; however, she caught on really quick, slurping them down as fast as we gave them to her.

# CHAPTER 13

## *Chinese Medicine*

We were prepared for it, but we didn't plan on it actually happening. The day before we were to fly south to complete our final leg of the journey, Samantha's fever spiked at 102.5° after her nap. She'd had a low grade temp off & on all week, which we thought may be related to teething. Such a high temperature made us a little more than nervous, so we called our guide, Cindy, who suggested we go ahead and take her to the doctor. I'm not sure which made us more uneasy: The fact her fever was spiking, or the realization were about to experience the application of Chinese medicine. We weren't really sure what was about to happen.

Cindy had the doorman of the hotel flag down a cab and off we went to the hospital. This was not a planned experience, but one worth writing about all the same. I thought perhaps we would go to some type of small clinic: Boy was I surprised. There is a Medical University Hospital in Lanzhou, so Cindy took us to the pediatrics department. Okay. I had taken out insurance for medical emergencies, plus brought a few thousand dollars and credit cards with me. I felt certain that we could handle most emergencies; this wasn't a major emergency, however, just a precaution against Samantha getting worse.

To begin, medical care is provided by the state in China, so there is no cost to the people who come to the hospital. Since this is a teaching hospital, most are treated by students and interns while supervised by the residents or professors. Thus, if you have money to pay a "donation" to the different departments, you get to go ahead of everyone else. So, that's what we did; actually, Cindy did that for us. Cindy told me on the way to the hospital, *"I'll take care of everything, and you can pay me back when we return to the hotel."* Okay.

We walked into the hospital and encountered lines that made the local DMV look small. I thought we'd be there until sometime the next week, yet, within about 10 minutes of arriving at the hospital, Samantha was already being examined. Cindy would point at a doorway or wall and tell us to wait, then went right to the window (in front of dozens of people standing in line), talk to the clerk, then open her wallet and hand them money. She would then collect us and repeat these actions at the next place. She told us to sit on a bench outside a treatment room on the second floor, and she went inside. Sixty seconds later, the mother and ten year old girl that were being treated in the room were being ushered out into the hallway by our guide. Cindy then turned to us, smiled and said, *"The doctor will see you now."* Okay. Leave it to Cindy; I guess the ability to circumvent long lines in a single bound is another one of her super-powers.

A professor of pediatrics examined Samantha quite thoroughly while two of his students looked on. He explained everything he was doing to them then allowed them to repeat his actions. As he tried to look down her throat, however, no one could get her to open her mouth. Oh how they tried with toys, funny faces and a variety of bizarre sounds. Yet, Samantha wouldn't budge. She was not amused. The doctor said something in Chinese which Cindy translated; *"He wants her to cry so he can look in her throat."* At that moment, Cindy, Debbie, the doctor, and the medical students all turned and looked at me! What's the Chinese word for "Whaaatttttt?" Okay, I'll be the meany: I just hope she's too young to remember this. I stepped forward and said her name really loud with a mean look on my face: That did it. I felt horrible. Did the daddy-daughter bond just disintegrate? Her bottom lip protruded, the big crocodile tears welled in her eyes, and she cried. What anguish and pain; and Samantha was crying too. I felt sooooooo bad! We'd spent all week bonding, and now I made her cry again. I need a hug.

As she began to cry and open her mouth, the doctor determined that Samantha had an acute infection in her throat. He'd also determined that her lungs were clear, so the doctor gave her an IV antibiotic, a topical breathing treatment to reduce the irritation, and prescribed an oral follow-up antibiotic. We now believe that maybe her low grade temp and drooling over the past couple of days may have been the beginning of this, and perhaps not teething as we had suspected. Yet again, our guide

Cindy proved astonishing. The doctor was very nice, and came by to check on Samantha while she was receiving the IV, which by the way was administered through a vein in her forehead. Needless to say, Samantha was not at all pleased, nor were we. They do this because of the activity of an infant- this was the only place we could keep the IV loaded without the potential of her jerking it out, and oh how she tried. The doctor decided on this course of treatment because we were flying out the next day and would not be able to do a return visit.

I should interject a word here about the conditions of the hospital: "Sterile" isn't a word I'll be using. One brief example: A little boy wearing split pants stopped in the middle of the hallway while Samantha was being examined. Split pants have an opening the length of the crotch and allow children who are potty training the ability to "go" anywhere, anytime. And, so this little guy stopped in the middle of the corridor and peed on the floor. When he was done, the boy and his mother continued on their way as if nothing had happened, despite the small puddle they'd left behind. About two minutes later, a woman came down the entire length of the hallway mopping the floor. When she got to the puddle, she just sloshed it around and kept going! Disgusting, but true. Don't know what else to say about the unsanitary conditions, so I'll leave it at that.

We were gone about two hours total, and Cindy stayed with us the entire time. What is even more astonishing is the fact that the total for medical care and taxi rides between the hotel and hospital was 130 yuan, or about $16 USD. Doctor, bribing the clerks to advance in the lines, the IV, and taxi: Sixteen dollars total. I wonder what they charge for Lasik surgery. We are thankful that Samantha was alright and will be healthy again soon, and even more thankful for our guide Cindy: I couldn't imagine attempting something like this by myself. By the time we went to dinner, Samantha was her usual self and we certainly felt better too! I told Debbie that since the cost of medical care was so cheap, we should go ahead and get Samantha a boob job for later: Debbie was not amused, but the rest of our group fell to pieces in laughter. I got Debbie's new expression again.

On a more serious note, there was another abandoned baby in the treatment room where Samantha got her IV. This baby boy was less than a month old and was born without a rectum. There he lay, all by himself on top of a cold stainless steel table. I wanted to go and hold him. I asked about the child and Cindy asked the nurse in the room. As she told me about the situation, Cindy was dialing the GWCA office in Beijing. The baby was in need of corrective surgery which the hospital will not do without a sponsor for the child, being that he was abandoned. Cindy left the room and asked if Great Wall China Adoptions will sponsor the operation. (Great Wall has a special program to help children with special needs). When she returned to the room, I asked Cindy later what would happen if they didn't get a sponsor, to which she became very stone faced and simply said, *"I can't talk about something like that."* I'm not sure what that meant, but it didn't sound good. Soon thereafter a nurse came and moved us into a room. It's hard for me to accept that the newborn baby I've just seen may die before we leave China; I wish there was something we could do. I wondered if someone could just hold this lonely little guy. I could not get him off of my mind. I asked how much it would cost to sponsor his surgery. Cindy asked the nurse, who went to ask someone else. We regrettably left the hospital without an answer.

When we returned to the hotel, the other families wanted to know about our experience which we shared during dinner. Truth be told, taking a trip to the ER or a doctor in a foreign country like China was the worst nightmare that most of us could think of. We told them about the other child that we'd seen, and a few of the group members made phone calls of their own. We never learned what happened to the little baby, but it was amazing to see the efforts made on his behalf. As I sent out emails to friends & family, two responded with questions about what they could do, so I put them in touch with our agency. To witness the magnitude of compassion for this little unknown child in China was astounding. All-in-all, it was a day to remember, not to mention our relief that Samantha was fine.

The experience also led me to reflect on the goodness of others. It has been a while since I was completely at the mercy of another person. I sat there beside my wife and daughter in that hospital feeling lost, alone, and helpless. Yet, that is where we found ourselves: In a Chinese hospital on the other side of the planet in the hands of a Chinese national named Cindy. We had to put complete trust in this young woman who was charged with looking out for the welfare of thirteen families. Even so, she acted as if we were her only concern. Her sense of urgency to get Samantha seen by a doctor would have led an observer to think Samantha was Cindy's own child. To watch this woman at work is to be amazed. At the end of our adventure, as we loaded the flight to head home, it is customary to give the guide a tip for her services. We looked at the recommended amount and then tripled it. Cindy was worth every penny, not only for her professionalism, but for her character – and her compassion.

To see the reaction of people on behalf of the other child, abandoned at the hospital, needing someone to intervene in order to live: I was again touched at how people responded. Even at home in Texas, people were ready to wire money for the little boy's surgery. Our trust in this adoption agency was indeed well placed. It seems to me our agency isn't just a handful of people doing a job. No, to the contrary: They are in the life changing business. They take pride, joy, and great delight in matching families with waiting children. I, for one, am truly amazed. During the rest of our trip, I kept looking for Cindy's wings; I know they must be there somewhere.

# CHAPTER 14

## *Homesick*

Merry Christmas and a Happy New Year! That's what we were all saying to each other this morning at breakfast, due to the seasonal tunes we've been listening to in the elevator & lobby of the hotel. I guess it's just another piece of music to the people here, but we frequently hear Silent Night, Ole Lang Sine, and other such holiday tunes (in June) playing in the elevator and over the intercom. Quite a peculiar mix of music to say the least. We were coming back from dinner on Thursday night, and as we waited for an elevator we heard Silent Night playing for the first time. All of us stopped talking and looked up at a speaker in the ceiling and started laughing.

The final leg of our journey in China has us back in Guangzhou for the final work to bring Samantha home. We woke Saturday morning at 4am to prepare to leave Lanzhou. The hotel kitchen manger had a buffet breakfast ready for our group at 5:00am, which is an hour earlier than usual for the hotel. Despite the cigarette smoke, filthy carpets, and dust that wreaked havoc on our allergies, it was a fairly decent hotel with a very devoted staff. We boarded the bus at 5:50am, and made the hour long ride to the airport to catch an 8:25 flight to Guangzhou. Once again, our guides checked our luggage for us an hour before we arrived at the airport, handed out tickets and boarding passes for us, and made getting on the flight very easy for us new parents. We said goodbye to our local guide, Steed Chen, and settled in for the 2.5 hour flight to Guangzhou.

I need to interject something about the in-China flights at this point. On our flight from Beijing and this flight to Guangzhou, our guides simply purchased the required number of tickets without consideration of having the seats together. Thus, when we boarded the plane, no-one in our group was sitting together. It wasn't that big a deal flying from Beijing to Lanzhou, but now that we all had infants it was not as humorous! Not to worry; our advocate, help, and defender of the faith "Cindy the Fierce" entered the plane and started moving the other passengers around so that most of the families could sit together. NO JOKE: She was actually telling other Chinese passengers to get up and move then redirecting us to sit together. I've been flying for thirty plus years and this was a first. Unfortunately, even the powerful Cindy could not get everyone seated together and such was our luck. Debbie and Samantha were a few rows back from where I was sitting, so I kept checking on them from time to time. I think I'll try that approach the next time I take a domestic flight in the US, and just order some passengers to move around for no reason! (I'll probably get glared at if I do)! What a hoot.

Samantha did quite well on her first airplane ride, although the descent was a bit tough on everyone's ears. A Chinese woman across the aisle took Samantha and played with her for about 10 minutes, which both seemed to enjoy. We left Lanzhou, a very nice, arid 42 degrees, and landed in Guangzhou to a balmy 84 degrees and high humidity. Still, it is great to be back were we started at the White Swan Hotel, knowing we are less than a week from returning home. After we were all liquefied by the heat and slid down the steps to the tarmac, we had the life sucked out of us while walking through the unventilated airport. As we finally boarded the bus to the White Swan, it was actually a good feeling to be back in familiar surroundings. We were ready to be home.

After we checked in, I retrieved a bag from the concierge we'd checked a week earlier, picked up an engraving of Samantha (from one of her pictures) we had started at a local shop, stopped by the 7-Eleven for diet coke & such, and dropped off the cameras that were sent to the orphanage 2 months ago (all of this in about 30 minutes). I also picked up a few little gifts to bring home that we had shopped on our previous stay and planned to buy on our return to Guangzhou. They have a great selection of "squeaky shoes" which we've been thinking about as well- that should really thrill our dogs. If you can stand the noise, I guess it's a good idea. It's also fun to watch the child's happy expression as she squeaks the shoes non-stop for about an hour.

For someone who enjoys Asian cuisine as much as I do, there is a point where you have to say: "Enough!" As it was about noon when we got to our room, we ordered delivery from a place that does American food called "Danny's Bagels." Their main menu is pizza, however they also have hot sandwiches like a Philly Cheese Steak, french fries, buffalo wings, potato skins, and all of those other bad things you need after two straight weeks of Chinese food. We collected clothes for the laundry and hand washed some items. A part of my new daily routine is preparing Samantha's medication and food for the next day, which I do each evening before her last bottle of the day. The only thing on our agenda remaining that day was to report for visa photos at 5pm- along with four other groups of adoptive parents. Fortunately, the photographer was at the same location as where I had dropped off the orphanage cameras, so as soon as our visa photos were complete, I picked up our seventy-two prints from the orphanage.

We are amazed that almost all of the photos are of Samantha, and a handful of the pictures include other children who were adopted by our group. The orphanage is very well run, and we have pictures of Samantha playing both inside and outside, standing in her crib, tooling around the playroom in a little walker, eating, and even having a tantrum. The nanny who handed her off to us is in most of the photos, and the ratio of nannies to children in all of the pictures appears to be 3 nannies per dozen kids, so not too bad. Additionally, the play room is decorated in a motif suitable for children with a blue half wall with trees, clouds, and little animals on the walls. We are very fortunate just to have these photos; I believe these will be valuable to Samantha later in life when she can comprehend the more abstract issues of her adoption. This was home for most of her first year.

Samantha has shown no fever twenty-four hours later, and she is once again the same glowing, happy, cheerful, and talkative little wonder that she had been previous to doctor's visit. We give her the oral antibiotic three times a day, which she has no problem taking. When we arrived at the hotel today, another family took their little girl to the clinic at the hotel for the same problem. They are also considering some elective procedures before we leave China.

The staff brought a crib to the room shortly after we arrived, which Samantha hates. She would rather have Debbie hold her all night. One thing we missed over the previous week was the wonderful shower and blanket sized towels at this hotel! Even though the water smells a little funny, you can't help but enjoy taking a shower a bit longer than usual. On Sunday, we complete the US visa application and submit it with the photos that were taken this evening. Monday, we hand in the visa application, pay that fee, and then take Samantha for a brief physical that afternoon which consists of a medical history review and weigh in. Tuesday we have a sight-seeing tour and lunch together, then a professional photographer will be here taking group and individual pictures. We bought swim diapers and a swim suit for Samantha to see if she likes the pool, so we'll try that Tuesday afternoon. On Wednesday we receive Samantha's passport with her US visa, then take an oath that we will provide Samantha with all the rights of a child living in the United States. As soon as that is over, it's back to the hotel to pack. Wednesday night we leave at 9pm to return to the States, returning to Los Angeles at 6pm pacific time the same day, then back to Houston the day after.

The past two weeks have been extraordinary. Visiting a foreign country we never imagined we would see, and the new sights, customs, and issues such an experience as this presents. Adopting a child and the culmination of all the multinational legal requirements involved. Most of all, we were now beginning an even greater journey: Becoming parents for the first time. I know that most of those who read this are already parents, grandparents, families who have also adopted from China, families who are waiting for referrals from China, and those who are curious. I'm sure that you parents and grandparents remember your reaction to finally holding your first child, whether conceived or adopted. The long period of preparation, waiting, and anticipating pales in comparison to that moment when that small, innocent, helpless being is first in our arms. To have their eyes look into yours, feel their heart beat as you hug them, hear with eagerness every little sound they make, and sense the awe in the deepest part of your being that a new relationship between parent and child has begun. It is beyond words for me, and we are both still in a bit of shock that she is actually ours: It seems like a dream. We're such a sight to behold; we get excited changing her diaper and can sit and stare at her sleeping for who knows how long. Tomorrow, I'm adding her to my health insurance and starting a payroll deduction for college. College tuition at the University of Tennessee should cost about as much as our house by then. Of course, with all the academic scholarships she'll receive as valedictorian . . .

I have to include one more note of cultural interest: Uniforms. Everywhere you go, it seems the people who work together have some sort of matching uniform. In America, that's expected at fast food restaurants and such places, but it happens almost everywhere here. Imagine walking into Dillard's and seeing all of the sales people dressed in lime green pants or skirts with a white shirt and a lime green tie or scarf. You think I jest, but 'tis true! The Bank of China, restaurants, shops, street cleaners, hotel staff, and on the list goes: They all wear matching uniforms. Not at every business, but at many of them. Just thought that was interesting.

# CHAPTER 15

## *When Dreams Come True*

It's time to come home!!! I feel a little like graduation: The end of one journey that transitions into the beginning of another. Family and friends are waiting to see this little bundle of joy for themselves. At last, we are a family! I know it will be some time before she learns to speak the word "daddy," but I can see it and sense it in her eyes. After one week together, she practically leaps into my arms, and she gets profoundly excited when we start playing games. I have a varied collection of music on my laptop, from classical to country, rock, pop, and Christian. Samantha listens to the tunes and starts bobbing back & forth. After a week of this, all you have to do is start singing and Samantha is bobbing along with you! Perhaps a future musician???

On Monday, we left after breakfast to go and see the Six Banyan Tree Temple in Guangzhou. This is an active temple with Buddhist monks. For a donation, they will even perform a "blessing" ceremony for the babies. They have a number of Buddha hanging around: The Buddha of Past, Present and Future in one temple; the Buddha of the lost peanut or something in another, and about six others I don't remember. Some of the braver souls climbed to the top of the main temple while the rest of us looked around the grounds. Lots of incense burning and many Chinese people worshiping. The six Banyan trees died many years ago, but the area still keeps that name. We watched as the monks blessed the adopted babies, but had no clue as to what he was saying. I asked our guide what the monk had said. She turned towards me, a cell phone on the opposite ear and said, "What monk?" Should have recorded it on video.

After the temple, we did our part to strengthen the local economy: We went to a large porcelain and jade retailer to help spend off our remaining foreign currency. Afterwards, we returned to the hotel in time for lunch. That afternoon, Samantha had to go for her required physical. Officially, she is only 16 pounds, and 28 inches long. (Tall and thin)! The physical was quite interesting. The Chinese doctor would look for the least little defect then give you every opportunity to reject the child. Of course, no one had any reservations whatsoever about the children we'd been given. Absolutely the most bizarre "physical" I've ever heard of.

We went out afterwards and picked up some more clothes that fit Samantha a little better, (everything we brought with us was a bit large). All of the shops around the White Swan Hotel have folks that speak English quite well. They are ready to barter with the Americans, and each shop has a tremendous variety of children's apparel. In addition to children's apparel, they have bolts of fabric and for about $20, they will make a jacket or blouse out of silk for you: Custom made! We each had an outfit made for us that we wore for our first family picture.

Believe it or not, I've also had my fill of Peking/Beijing Duck and all other dishes Chinese on this trip. With such a heavy diet of Chinese cuisine, even though it was really great Chinese food, a cheese steak and fries at this point is like a filet mignon with a loaded baked potato. Okay; you can stop with the jaw dropping now. By the way, Samantha has been introduced to french-fries: I think it's her new favorite food.

As we turn our attention to preparing to head home, we hope the disruption in schedule and twenty-plus hours in flight to Houston will not be too much for Samantha. Of course, getting to this point with her has helped prepare us to care for her during the flight home, so we think it will be alright. Samantha is very ticklish around her feet, knees, and ribs, and we have great fun tickling her. She laughs hysterically then stares at you with a smile anticipating that we'll tickle her again. I sang "Old McDonald" for about an hour last night to entertain her, which encompassed dozens of animals. (Good thing I watch the Discovery Channel frequently). She loves for me to be silly and seems to have a lot of fun with songs like that. She also likes the "hand spider." I put my fingers down and use them as legs while my hand crawls around. Eventually it crawls up and over her body and head then tickles her ribs. She laughs quite loud then stares at my hand until I do it again. All three of us have bonded quite well during the last eleven days. Notwithstanding the first night that I was left alone with her and the whole IV in the head thing, Samantha has a very charming, pleasant and sweet disposition.

Our last day in China, we were to have some professional photographs made, however, the photographer had a wreck on the way due to the rain and the photos were canceled. (This part of southern China is tropical, and we have something just short of a typhoon coming in). So, everyone wound up taking their own photos with their own cameras, which was very hectic. Not to worry, "hectic" would be the word of the day as we prepared to return home.

Wednesday afternoon, we picked up Samantha's passport at about 3pm. Our luggage, now up to four suitcases and four carry-on pieces, went ahead of us to the airport about 5pm, and we departed the hotel at 6pm- just ahead of some major thunderstorms. After being glared for the last time by security, we finally got to rest for a while before boarding. We have been anxiously waiting to see if another couple we met this week will make this flight. They are with another adoption agency, and when we left the hotel, their guides were still not back with the babies' passports and visas. Since they've already been checked out of the hotel, their luggage is here at the airport and this is the only flight back to the US tonight. I shudder to think of what they face. Just one more affirmation that we chose the right agency.

Our guides have been astonishing: Ultimate professionals who really know what they are doing. I guess it really makes a difference when the guides are employed by the Agency. Many of the other people here are in the hands of third party guides that work for numerous state agencies, travel offices, and so forth. In conversations each day over breakfast, the difference in service is significant. We frequently hear- *"Our guides didn't do that- we had to figure it out for ourselves."* When you don't speak the language, and you are that far away, a great guide is priceless!

After almost three weeks in China, we are really looking forward to getting back home. As international travel goes, this is the longest trip we've ever made and we are glad it is coming to an end. There are many conveniences of home that we miss (washer, dryer, fridge, our dogs, water that's not contaminated by significant bacteria), but most of all we long to get Samantha home into her new world and family. We can't wait for everyone to meet her! This Sunday is Father's Day in the United States, but for me- Father's Day has been every day since I first held our baby. It's been interesting and fun seeing different parts of China, both ancient and contemporary, and we have enjoyed everything except the food poisoning. What an extraordinary people and culture: I just wonder what our culture will be like after our nation has been around for five thousand years. Anyway, our journey is at the same time ending and just beginning.

It is now 8pm, and we will begin boarding soon, so I'll end my travel journal at this point. There is still no sign of the missing family; I guess they'll miss the flight. Anyway, as we prepare to say goodbye to China, let me quote that great philosopher and guru of wisdom- Dorothy of Oz- and say on behalf of Debbie and myself: "*There's no place like home.*"

**Saying goodbye. Cindy holds Samantha one
last time in the Guangzhou Airport**

# CHAPTER 16

## Home Coming: A New Journey Begins

We are back home; Unpacked, recovering from jet lag, and introducing Samantha to her new home and family. I wish I could say that our final 24 hour flight home was uneventful, but when flying a certain Houston based airline, that just doesn't seem possible. Of all the airlines I've ever flown, they are hands-down and unequivocally the worst I've experienced (horror stories galore). As far as we were concerned, they'd certainly lived up to their low standards once again. Being treated so well by Delta and the various Chinese carriers, it is quite the contrast in rudeness and apathy that brought us from Los Angeles back to Houston for our final flight.

I'll start by confirming that the families I mentioned previously with a certain other agency didn't make the flight, which means they had to spend two extra days in Guangzhou without their luggage. I can't stress enough how important it is to have a solid, professional, and well established adoption agency working with you. GWCA was outstanding, especially in taking care of us while in China. (*For those of you considering a different agency, you need to ask who will be representing you in China- employees of the agency or the lowest bidding third party contractor*).

While waiting for our flight, we realized we still had a few hundred Yuan left (about $45) which would be worthless back home. After Debbie collected one of each bill for our scrapbook, I was off to the airport shops to pick up some snacks and last minute stuff. Among the items I purchased were two black T-shirts for Samantha with white Mandarin writing. When

Debbie asked me what the writing said, I responded; "Made in China." She and our travel companions were amused. For all I know, it could mean "Born to Poop."

We boarded China Southern, departed promptly at 9pm, and were pampered and cared for by their devoted staff during the 15 hour flight to Los Angeles. It's also truly amazing how polite, courteous, and professional these flight attendants are who make about $2,000 per year, compared to our U.S. flight staff making twenty times that amount with their limited customer service skills. I also need to mention that there were about three dozen families on the flight who had also adopted from China. The first half of the flight occurred during the time that the babies would normally be sleeping in China, so it was fairly quiet and uneventful on board- (meaning nothing happened to wake me up). We arrived in Los Angeles about 6:45pm Pacific Time- right on schedule.

As we entered the customs area from baggage claim, the customs officer at the door asked how many adoptive families were on the plane. When I said "three to four dozen," she rolled her eyes and said, "Oh Lord!" While standing in line, I was wondering what would have happened if I'd said what I was actually thinking- (*Oh, the whole plane is nothing but two hundred adoptive families- it was a specially chartered flight*). The poor woman would have probably had a stroke. As it was, it took right at an hour for us to clear customs. Apparently the US Customs office in Los Angeles has only one person who knows how to handle this extra paperwork. After about 40 minutes, there were nine empty customs booths. Then there was ours with a line out the door and into the baggage claim.

When we received our initial itinerary, I arranged a stay at a nearby hotel for our return to the U.S.: The Four Points Sheraton LAX. We preferred to break the trip up to gain our bearing, care for Samantha, and start recovering from the long flight. Of course, the original itinerary also had us landing in Houston at 6am and up all night. Not knowing how our new child would handle the flights, we thought breaking up the flight was the best course of action.

It was also past dinner time for us when we arrived at the hotel, so as we entered the hotel parking lot around 8pm, we eye-balled the restaurants nearby: (I was to go forage for food and bring back my kill). When we arrived in our room, however, another surprise awaited us. There on the table was a card from my dad welcoming us back home, along with a prepaid room service tab for dinner. Wow, what a wonderful thing to do! We had talked on the ride in about how much we both craved a fresh salad: So we ordered a couple of salads . . . along with the evening special of prime rib, loaded baked potato, freshly baked rolls, shrimp cocktail, and some wonderful cheesecake. With such a meal consumed, the only available option is to pass out and sleep.

We were able to sleep a little while in the hotel, however, as Samantha had been sleeping for the past ten hours, she was ready to play! She also hated the crib, so she slept on the bed with us; Or should I say she flopped around on the bed while we tried to sleep. Still, it was good to have 16 hours to lay down and rest following the hectic and busy final days of our trip, and Samantha did end up taking a four hour nap so that we could sleep too (she's very considerate like that). Now we were ready to be home. I ordered some breakfast and after packing up again we headed back to the airport.

We've flown almost every US carrier there is, as well as most of the major international airlines. There are some airlines that really take pride in what they do and how they treat you. The Chinese airlines were hands down some of the most customer friendly airlines I've ever flown. Then there are certain airlines that seem annoyed and irritated that they have to deal with the public. The flight attendants don't look up at you, never make eye contact, and tend to walk away as quickly as possible the minute you ask a question (pretending as if they never saw you). I think they must send all their customer service reps to a special training class to learn how to be this unhelpful. No collective group of human beings can be this inept without expert help.

We boarded the airline in Los Angeles for the final leg, and with the help of some Crisco and a really large shoe spoon, I finally made it into my anorexic super-model seat. I did, however, have to store my legs in the overhead compartment as there was no room for them between my seat and the one in front of me. After flying on seven different aircraft over the past two weeks, I can tell you with all certainty that the carrier we flew on the final leg is the master of squeezing every possible seat they can onto their planes: Passenger comfort is definitely not a consideration. I think they'd have stacked seats on top of each other if they could get away with it. I knew I was in trouble when I saw their first class seats were the same size as every other airlines' economy class seats. The coach section looked like two hundred infant booster chairs jammed together. As bad as this was, I was also the lucky fella who got to sit behind the jerk determined to see how horizontal he can make his chair move. I'm not exaggerating here: When he plopped his seat backwards, the top of his chair was pressed against my chest. Of course, I don't know why he was so startled when I forcibly returned his seat to its full and upright position. Maybe it was because I catapulted him into the cockpit door from row twenty-two, but I can't be sure about that.

Also consistent with my previous experiences with this carrier, we were late for departure. Had they lost our luggage I'd have felt perfectly at home: The bad service trifecta! What words can I use to express my joy of being a flesh sandwich for that additional hour on the tarmac, nestled in a polyester kiddie chair that had not been cleaned in years. I could ramble onward about how I loathe this airline, but I don't know that many vile and contemptible words. I know. Such words and attitude from a minister. Forgive my human nature. I guess it's the one thing that really gets me – professional rudeness. There are some wayward people in life for whom you have low expectations: To be treated rudely by them is no shock. But to have someone representing a customer service profession who clearly despises customers, that's a real sore spot in my book. 'Nuff said. Soapbox smashed.

Approximately four hours later, we bounced repeatedly onto a runway in Houston around 7pm. Stunned that the pilots had not only found Texas but the correct airport as well, we rejoiced in hushed tones as we exited the aircraft with jubilant mooing and bleating. Of course, being late has additional consequences: Instead of exiting the aircraft about 100 yards from the baggage claim entrance as planned, we were banished to disembark at a terminal on the Texas-Louisiana border. After literally walking for 30 minutes, we arrived at the escalator that would take us down to the baggage claim.

As I entered the escalator, I saw Debbie's sister at the bottom bouncing with excitement. Within a few seconds, other friends and family members gathered at the base of the moving steps to welcome us home. My oh my, what a homecoming! There were painted banners welcoming Samantha to the USA and everyone was waving U.S. flags. Debbie's mom was filming our arrival with a digital camcorder while others took photos. (That was good, considering I was too tired to even look for my camera). I've never been hugged so much in my life- and I enjoyed every minute of it! As I reached the bottom of the escalator, I moved out of the way so everyone could finally meet Samantha face to face.

She was immediately surrounded by a couple dozen people, which she took in stride. She was passed around and held by almost everyone there and she didn't seem to mind too much. Grandparents, aunts, uncles, cousins, and friends: Everyone was eager to say hello and hold this little gem. While I talked with friends about the trip, it was so powerful just to step back and watch others experience what we had gone through a couple of weeks earlier when we got to hold her for the first time. Samantha gave everyone lots of smiles & giggles, and accepted kisses, hugs, and a couple of bears from the room full of strangers. She did look a little puzzled as if she were trying to figure out what all the fuss was about.

**Samantha's Homecoming in Houston>>**

By the time we collected our luggage and started for the door, I realized we had been there in the baggage claim for over an hour. In fact, ours was the only luggage still by the baggage claim belt. We all decided to stop at a Mexican restaurant on the way home to continue the celebration. We shared things about our trip, ate, laughed, and talked until well after 10pm. I don't know anything as heartwarming and memorable as a wonderful homecoming. Yet, that was the culmination of sharing this process for the last year and a half with those who were there. They had been with us from the beginning.

**Captain's Log; Stardate 061804.** (I've always wanted to do that). Well . . . this is it: The actual end of this story - almost. I wanted to write a few words about finally walking into our house and the wonderful relief of being home. I've been sitting here for a couple of hours re-reading the journal entries and emails sent while in China, and enjoyed looking at the hundreds of pictures from our trip. I'm sure eventually all that has transpired will begin to sink in. For now, it seems we are still living the dream.

So, if you'll indulge me to share a final story before I talk about more serious things, I'll draw this tale to a close. This morning, we all awoke a little after 3am, so it was off to grab an early breakfast and then on to the grocery store to replenish our fridge. Once we returned home and finished unpacking, I headed to the kennel to collect our dogs who were equally bursting with excitement after nearly 3 weeks away from us. Introducing Samantha to our dogs was in our mind the final leg of being home, and it was quite something to behold.

We have three miniature schnauzers, ranging in age from 2 years to 10 years. The oldest, Cozette, after one glance and a disinterested sniff wasn't very impressed with Samantha and promptly moved on to lie down on the sofa. The youngest, Sheba- who usually acts as if severely brain damaged- sniffed Samantha up and down then started looking for something else to play with. Sparky, the six year old male was the only dog really interested. He sniffed her repeatedly and stayed very close by. He sat down and stared at Samantha, and she stared back at him. This was Samantha's first experience seeing a live animal, so she was exhibiting a number of reactions: Excitement, curiosity, trepidation, and that look we deem to be "puzzled." Since Sparky was the only one who didn't run away, Samantha sat on my lap in wide eyed wonder looking at him. Sparky, showing his usual amount of affection, gingerly stepped forward inch by inch. Once he had reached within a couple of inches of Samantha, he nosed forward and gave her a great big slobbering lick on the lips! Samantha was a bit alarmed by this, but in good stride decided to return the favor. She grabbed Sparky by the beard with both hands, leaned forward, stuck out her tongue and licked him back across the mouth. Sparky seemed a bit shocked, and I started laughing and howling until I couldn't see straight. I guess it made quite an impact on Sparky: He has not left Samantha's side since. Anywhere she goes, Sparky is right behind her. Yes, I think we are home at last, and all is well in the world.

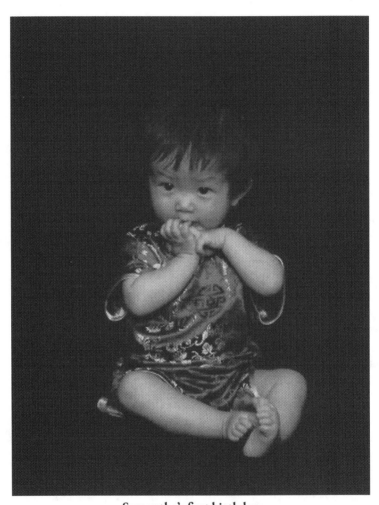

Samantha's first birthday

# CHAPTER 17

## *Life's More Serious Questions*

It was only a movie; fiction based upon truth. The ritual of allowing the more popular students to pick their teams. A painful debasement of those who remain after the initial choices have been made and the bargaining begins. Their peers call them losers, dregs. Standing against the gym wall, staring at their feet, wishing the pain of this moment would end. Shifting feet, chin in chest, visible emotional discomfort. Made to feel insignificant, worthless. They would vanish into thin air if possible. The degrading knowledge that you are unwanted and deemed unworthy. Deafening humiliation. Such rejection haunts the psyche for years, even a lifetime.

I've seen it in real life as well. In the office as a woman disclosed the agony of finding her husband no longer desired her. In the aftermath of a suicide, convinced beyond hopelessness that their pain would ever cease. In the questions of the adopted. It is the one concern that I am prepared to face someday when her cognitive skills can process such abstract concepts. Deep within, I hope she never asks. Why did my parents not want me? Why was I rejected by the one who gave me birth? Did they not love me? Did they not need me? How could they abandon me, leaving me with strangers? Is there something wrong with me? I will have some answers. Will those responses suffice? I cannot tell her with certainty what I do not know. I cannot take her where I have not been. I selfishly hope that her relationship to us never gives her doubt.

Until that day she becomes independent from us, we will continue to prepare for the questions. We have compiled documents, data, and evidence. We can prove it was the government which forced her parent's choice. Our answers center upon the contention that her parents would have done anything to keep her if they could have. It's called the "One Child Policy." It was implemented in 1979 to help begin controlling government costs for supplying state sponsored welfare. While it primarily applies to less than forty percent of the nation- mainly those living in the more densely populated urban areas, there are rules and exceptions. Rural families can have two children with certain provisions; however, they are paid an additional stipend for having only one child, (around $100 a year or more, depending upon their occupation). Urbanites who have more than one child can find themselves facing a "tax" which tends to be one hundred times their annual salary. We clipped one article in which a woman in Hunan earning $1,240 per year was fined $124,000 for keeping a second child. Other stories from various news organizations in China have reported penalties to include unemployment, rescinding all state sponsored welfare, and even locking the family & their relatives out of their homes; (Even if people own their own homes, the People's Republic of China still holds claim to all land). We have evidence of these things, but will that really matter?

We'll never know the exact reasons that her parents abandoned her, but we can speculate with some certainty. We will argue hope. In a life and business in which I have studied and learned to read people by their behavior, I will present my findings to my child about her biological mother. Yet, will it be enough? We will never know the identity of her biological parents. The evidence is scarce, but there is some. Like small pieces of a puzzle that begin to suggest a greater picture, that which we know tells us it was a hard decision for them; an extremely hard decision. Based on what we know, I dream of that morning often. What happened on that summer morning when her biological mother walked away? Here is my conjecture based on what we know:

In the small city of Zhangye just south of the Gobi desert, the hushed hues of amber pushed against the night sky, revealing the first glimmer of dawn approaching the horizon. She watched the transition between day and night as she held her sleeping child, but sleep did not come this night for her. The early morning air was cool and dry, common for such an arid climate. It is August 7th, 2003. It will be fair and dry today; Rain would give her at least one more day with her baby. How she prayed it would rain.

As a piece of her heart slowly died within her, she dressed her second child for the last time in an additional layer of clothing, not knowing how long it would take for someone to find her. New clothes, a very common outfit purchased specifically for this day. Hand-me-downs from her firstborn might cause someone to recognize who was behind this act. She could not risk being discovered. A tear fell on her sleeping girl's cheek as she kissed her one more time. Her husband and older daughter lay sleeping. The time had come.

It had been one month, and they could no longer keep up the ruse. The cost of being discovered would be devastating; the options are few. She knows that others like her have done the unthinkable: Placing the child in the nearby woods immediately after birth, the blood covered newborn attracting the animals that would leave no trace. She is much stronger, much braver. She has planned this day carefully. She has stolen every moment she could. And yet, it has been four weeks, and each day has made it all the more difficult to part from her beautiful, sleeping angel. She tells herself that if there is hope for her family and this child, it is in giving up the one that all may survive.

She thinks back to the Lunar New Year as they celebrated in the center of town. She could feel this new life growing within her body. They prayed earnestly it would be a boy. That one who would be their salvation in their old age. A child they would be able to legally keep. She could not go to the hospital for an ultrasound; her secret would have been revealed. Only during birth would they know. This pregnancy was even carefully concealed from their first born daughter, one too young to know what was at hand, too young to reveal her mother's condition. She dressed in fuller clothing to hide her condition as long as possible, then feigned illness and missed work at the end to conceal the final weeks. "It's a girl," were the words in hushed tones. They had already determined what they would do.

She prepares a bottle and closes the remaining bag of milk powder, placing it in the box. She then lifts her little girl into this makeshift, cardboard crib along with the bottle. She pulls the small blanket around her, kissing her once more before shielding her baby's face. Mustering all of her courage, she departs for her destination, praying this child will not awaken and reveal her secret.

For the last few weeks, she has considered multiple choices. The police station in Zhangye is too busy, too unpredictable. Too much risk of being discovered. She is known in the city; she cannot risk doing this while the shops are open. She staked out other locations, learning patterns of movement so as to take advantage of the most opportune moment for both of them. Her choice was no accident; no random selection. A well conceived plan for a heartbreaking purpose.

A woman moves unseen through the parking lot. Soft and careful steps; not wanting to be heard, not wanting to awaken her precious cargo. The night shift was about to end in less than an hour, the day shift set to begin arriving. It is still, quiet, peaceful. With quickness and stealth, she places the box just inside the gate of the employee parking area. She has watched in the days before as employees funnel through this narrow passage and across the drive into the People's Hospital of Zhangye. It offered hope that one of the hospital staff could not help but notice this odd obstacle in their path.

Her mind racing, she places her final kiss upon that soft cheek; it is almost more than she can bear. She pulls herself away with determination and resolve. She slips into the shadows, hidden in secret, watching, softly crying, wanting to make sure her daughter is taken inside. Though her heart is breaking, she continues assuring herself she has no other choice. A distant light breaks her train of thought. A car approaches, stops, crosses the street and enters the lot. It pulls into a reserved space. The lights fade as the engine dies. A car door closes and the soft steps of a woman are heard moving towards the hospital. It is a nurse supervisor arriving early to prepare for her shift. The mother in hiding stands upright to gain a better view.

The woman stops. She looks in the basket. She is motionless. She bends down to get a better look then stands abruptly in surprise. She turns again towards the entrance and hastily disappears inside the building. The mother in secret is distraught, disappointed, until she hears something else. The woman has returned with another employee, this one a doctor in manner of dress. She cannot make out what they are saying, but feels such relief as the doctor kneels and places his hands in the box. He shakes the baby to awaken her. The cries of her child are soft, and grow louder. The doctor nods in affirmation, then gently cradles the box and carries it inside. She exhales in great relief. Her child is safe. The plan has succeeded. She can return home. She will tell no one. She will carry this moment for the rest of her life.

We know from the reports what happened to the child from that point onward. The infant girl was taken to the maternity ward for keeping and observation until the authorities arrived. The police took the nurse's statement then called for the Zhangye Social Welfare Institute to come and retrieve the child. By noon she was given a physical at her new home. Judging by the fair complexion and appearance, the child is of local heritage and of northern Chinese ancestry. The police issued their typical notice in the local paper. They had ascertained from her condition that she was only a month old, and assigned her date of birth as July 8, 2003. The official notice states that a baby was found in a box, wearing this outfit, with these items, on this date, at this time and location. After two months with no one responding to claim the child, she officially became a ward of the government. Following a complete physical at five months old, she was deemed fit to become one of the very few who would be eligible for adoption. Her dossier was completed and forwarded to the Chinese Council for Adoption Affairs. In time, she was matched with us.

What we don't know is what happened to her family after that point. When I consider what I know of her area and the laws of the land, I have more questions than answers. Was this the first time her mother had given up a child? Most often, the second and additional daughters are abandoned, so it stands to reason my daughter has a big sister, maybe now even a brother. Holding onto a child for a month is uncommon. Most children are abandoned within the first few days following birth. Why did she hold on this long? Was the baby sick or premature: She was only six and a half pounds after thirty days. Did she need that much time to gain her strength? A sick or premature child would not be considered for placement. A less than adequate child may not even be allowed to live.

Or could it be a mother's love that fought for every minute she could get with her child before making this sacrifice? Did she fight every moment of every day against the inevitable, drinking in every nuance of her baby? The new clothing, packaged milk powder from a local store, and plastic bottle lead me to believe that this woman lived within the city, perhaps even within walking distance of the hospital. We have a picture of the hospital, the parking lot, and the gate where Samantha was abandoned. Reading about the others in the Zhangye SWI, most were wrapped in old and worn rags or hand-made clothing, and abandoned away from the city center. A child this young would have more than likely been breast fed if she lived outside of the city, not bottle fed. Everything about this abandonment tells me that her mother wanted this child to be found. Her circumstances tell me her birth mother loved her very much. I have no proof, yet little doubt that she watched from a distance until her little one was safe. Still, the questions linger in my mind.

The first time I saw her picture, then only five months old, my arms longed to hold her. The day I first held her, nothing could have torn her from me. She looked into those eyes for a month. She held those little hands for weeks. She sang the first songs my daughter ever knew. Is my daughter's mind haunted by the voice of a woman she does not remember?

She watched over her sleeping angel long before I did. She held my daughter, their hearts beating as one. She gave her countless kisses for thirty days, knowing they would have to last her daughter a lifetime. Does she still keep that special blanket that cradled her little one for a month? Does she breathe in her fragrance and long for her baby? Does she wonder what her daughter looks like now? Do her arms still ache today to hold her? What did she name her? I feel certain that my daughter had a name: No mother could hold onto a child for a month and not name her I tell myself.

Did she secretly spy on the Zhangye SWI, trying to catch a glimpse of her baby? Did she have a contact within that place that told her which children were being taken to the Americans for adoption? I think of those things that I would have done. Would she have done the same?

I would love to have more answers. I will never know the whole truth, and to that regret, neither will my little girl. If we could return to Zhangye and scout out all of the schools, would I see a girl so similar to my daughter in appearance, that I would know it was Samantha's sister? Would I see Samantha's features in a woman on the street; a woman with distant and longing eyes?

These are the questions that occasionally frequent my mind. And still I imagine what I would say if I could meet this woman face to face for just a moment. I would thank her for the astonishing gift she has given us. I know her life changed that day when she walked away from her baby. Our lives also changed that day.

I would want her to know that we see in those eyes all that she saw that lone month. I would assure her that everything she could dream for her baby, we will make a reality. Most of all, I would want to express that we love our little girl: Hers and ours. Two families on opposite sides of the planet connected by one small, precious life.

I would want to leave her with a thousand pictures of Samantha growing up in Texas, but fear it would be too overwhelming to consider what she has lost. I look at my daughter, now peacefully asleep as I write, and cannot imagine a life without her. I would not want a life without her. All I can do at this point is pray and prepare for the time when Samantha begins to ask these things in earnest. On August 7th of each year I pray for a courageous woman whom I've never met. I owe her so much. I know I will ever discover her identity; she made sure of that. By her capitulation, she has changed our lives. I wish there was something I could do to bring peace to her family. I pray that somehow God will fill the awesome void that must be hers. I pray that He will fill her with peace, somehow certain that her little angel is in loving arms. I pray that final kiss upon her daughter's cheek will forever linger on her lips. I pray that for her sacrifice, God will give her a son. Amen.

# CHAPTER 18

## *Conclusion: Father to Father*

That's our story. I love telling it. I get such a rush out of re-reading those life changing events and remembering. As my daughter grows older each year, we realize more and more that we are blessed beyond measure. None-the-less, this part of our story- the beginning- must come to a close. We will add it to the videos and photos of my daughter's life. The original manuscript will be hers. We decided to publish it as a story of faith and human interest. When asked by a potential agent to summarize the book, I said; "It's about the most important things in life: Love, family, and belonging. It's the fantastic journey to become a family through Chinese adoption as told by a father." I was surprised when after a moment of silence the agent said; "Actually, I know someone personally who is in the process of adopting a little girl from China; how soon can you send me the manuscript? I'd like to read that."

Our daughter is now six. My wife and I still watch her sleeping each morning and awaken her with kisses and gentle tickles. Our hearts are still as full as the day she was first placed in our arms. I pray and wish that everyone could know the love we have as a family. Maybe it's because our longing went unanswered for so long that we appreciate this child so deeply, but I have hope that every parent knows this love I'm writing about.

Other parents have told me, after listening to how I speak of my daughter; "You're still in the honeymoon phase- wait until she's a teenager!" I understand what they mean. As a pastor & therapist, I've counseled the families of pregnant teens, parents of adolescents in the ER detoxifying, and in those devastating events which led to a funeral home as they worked through the arrangements for their child. I've seen the bewildered disbelief in their eyes as they try to contemplate the choices their children have made, and remember the many times my own parents rolled their eyes as their boys made inexplicable decisions. I've taught parenting classes to moms and dads sentenced to my course by a judge, due to excessive truancy, juvenile incarceration, and young lives out of control. These observations and experiences tell me as a parent, I truly do not know what tomorrow holds. Each day is an investment with no guarantee as to the outcome.

Of course, I watch my increasingly independent child and wonder about her choices and future. One Wednesday evening, a fellow pastor who adopted a girl from China caught his beautiful, intelligent, yet strong willed eight year old baptizing some of her little friends in the church baptistery. He was not amused. All of the children were stark naked; they were afraid they'd be in trouble if they got their clothes wet. I wish I could have been there as he explained his daughter's actions to the other parents; I may need to know that someday. In terms of eight year old logic, it makes perfect sense. When she was four, Samantha did what she'd seen her daddy do and baptized most of her dolls in the bathtub. I put on the breaks when she wanted to dunk the dozens of pandas in her collection, despite her assurance that after a while in the clothes dryer they'd be just fine. I wonder when someone will come and find me at church to say, "You'll never believe what you're daughter is doing in the baptistery." That, I can live with, yet I wonder if I'll ever have one of those life shattering phone calls that no parent should ever get. No guarantees.

A grandmother in our church with custody of her teen granddaughter emailed me a joke that I have hanging on my wall. It's about a seventy year old widowed woman who went to her doctor and asked for birth control pills. The doctor looked at her a bit bemused and asked her to repeat the request. After hearing her again, he asked, "Are you telling me that you are still able to bear children at your age?" In explanation, she told the doctor that the birth control pills helped her sleep at night. The doctor started telling her about other medicines that would be much better for helping her sleep, but the woman refused. She told the doctor, "I have custody of my sixteen year old granddaughter and the birth control pills are for her: I put them in her coffee each morning, and I sleep much better at night!"

I can understand why the lady in my church likes that joke. We all want the best for our children, and we're competing for their love, understanding, attention, and direction in a self-indulgent, self-centered & distracting world that doesn't care about them. She'll see movies and television programs that endorse ungodly, perverted, and repulsive values. She'll spend fifteen years or more surrounded by other kids, (some of whom will not be the sharpest tools in the shed), who will tell her that what she and her parents believe is nonsense. They'll entice her to try and deceive her parents, to "experiment," and they'll attempt to manipulate her into compromising her integrity and character for a fleeting moment of frivolity. She's currently in first grade and it's already happening. If that foresight doesn't' drive a parent to their knees, I don't know what would. It makes me realize that I need help; not just any help, but help from the greatest Father I know.

So, for this final chapter, and as a man of deep faith, I want to talk about love. Not the giddy, romantic kind of love, but a deeply abiding, completely satisfying love. A love beyond what I feel for my wife and daughter. It's about the love that my heavenly Father has for me – and you too. As a "postlogue," I have learned more about my heavenly Father by becoming Samantha's daddy. Not only did adopting Samantha make me a dad, but it helped me understand so much more about being a son. I see that love now in my own father's eyes and in the fond memories of all he did for my brothers and me when we were children. I'm sure that more than once, our collective behavior and individual decisions drove him to his knees. No guarantees indeed.

As I ponder the growing love that I have for my daughter, I know that there is nothing I would not do for her. Yes, I am "wrapped." Gladly so. She's so loveable, precious, and she needs me. The bond we share as father and daughter is quite powerful. We have a connection beyond anything I've ever experienced. I'm sure that someday her independence and self-sufficiency will render me irrelevant, but for now, I am her daddy; a huge part of her world. She is undoubtedly a large part of mine.

After reading this book, I don't think anyone would doubt my love for Samantha. So considering all that we have gone through to adopt our daughter, could you imagine me sacrificing her for someone else? Can't wrap your head around something that tragic? Neither can I. To lose her for any reason is beyond imagination; certainly it is not something I dwell upon. My life as her father is consumed with helping her learn, watching her grow, and helping her become the woman she will be tomorrow. And yet, I have entered the homes of too many parents who have lost a child. No parent should ever have to bury a child, but that is our reality. To lose a child is the most painful loss I've ever witnessed. So how could our Heavenly Father do that?

I've considered over the last few years the death of Jesus on the cross. Did God still see the face of His little boy looking up from the manger? I think of Mary there witnessing the agonizing death of her first born son. The Bible records a man so compassionate and tender in healing the hurts of all He encountered; now He hangs dying such a vicious and cruel death. No mercy. No help. No relief. Such an event is beyond unbearable. Mary must have felt sickened to her core. It must have been heartbreaking in heaven as Jesus died on the cross. God, by encasing Himself in flesh, experienced first-hand the sting of death, and the despair that accompanies loss. The gospel accounts state that darkness fell upon the earth as Jesus was crucified: Why wouldn't darkness encompass the land- they were extinguishing the Light of the World. Jesus cried out, *"Father, Father; why have you forsaken me?"* God turned away. So would I; I couldn't bear to watch my child endure such pain.

He turned away because of love. How could God look at His only begotten Son in pain, agony, and approaching death, covered and filled with the sins of mankind that only He could bear? As a parent, my life would mean nothing if it meant taking away my daughter's pain. And yet God allowed his Son to die; His Father allowed the pain. I really do love my little girl: What's not to love? ***And yet, the greatest love I can express for this little girl pales in comparison to the love that God has for us!*** That's right. My intense love for my little girl is NOTHING compared to the love that God has for each of us. He loved us enough to do the unthinkable. He desired to claim us as children so much, He allowed the suffering, agony, and death of His child in exchange to make us His children. That was the price. Such was the cost. And God offers this gift of adoption to anyone who will say yes!

Some woman, somewhere in central China gave up her baby, and in doing so allowed our dreams to come true. Despite my understanding of China's one child policy, it is still incomprehensible to me that any mother would willingly give up her baby. Yet, God did so much more. He gave His only Son so that we might be adopted too. Imagine that: God's greatest desire – is for us! He allowed the unthinkable, gave up His most treasured creation, all for us. The paperwork has been completed, the price has been paid. Before all humanity, God offers us a new and eternal family. We can be adopted too.

My daughter didn't have a choice; that's one difference in the parallel. We did all the work for her and we paid 100% of the price. God has done the same for us. He has done all the work, He has paid the price, and He has prepared a place for us. He will someday call us home to be with Him. Until then is the waiting period.

I continue to clip articles about life in China; news stories from throughout China that will help her understand things about her heritage. I like to think that if she knew the life of hard labor and work with little benefit or privilege that awaited her had she remained in the orphanage in China, I'm sure she would have dreamed away her childhood wishing that someone would adopt her. Millions of children in China face that very thing. Yet, God gives us that choice. He offers to become our Father. He offers us the opportunity to become one of His children. Why? Because of a love more profound, intense, and real than I can express. I can feel that love, because I said yes to His grand offer, but it was when I became bonded to this little girl that I first started to see the passion of the father/child relationship that God desires to know with us.

It is with a deeply profound joy that I can say "I know love." I am fortunate to have parents, a wife, and a daughter who love me through & through. My understanding of love was amplified through the experience of adopting my daughter. I can now envision just a glimpse of how God the Father looks at us. It is truly amazing to know such a deep and satisfying love. Father to father, I am overwhelmed. Like David in Psalm 139, I want to say, "*It is too wonderful for me to understand.*"

You may have picked up this book because you are considering adoption. My prayers go with you. All the same, if you've never been adopted into God's family, then you're missing out on the greatest joy possible. Your heavenly Father wants you as much as you want a child; even more so. Wouldn't you like to be adopted too? Wouldn't you like to be a part of God's family? In Deuteronomy thirty-two, verse 11, Moses describes God's nurturing love for His children as a grand eagle, making its nest and spreading its majestic wings around them for protection and comfort. He is not some distant, far off God, but a very tender, loving, and involved Father. It is no wonder that more than seventy-two times in the gospel narratives, Jesus referred to God with the familiar and intimate word "Father."

God's offer is open to all who will accept it. Our Father waits with deep longing for each of us, waits for us to either accept His love or reject it. When you come to understand the greatest love ever demonstrated; More importantly, when you come to accept it and receive it, it changes you forever; a spiritual "defining moment." Imagine being able to say, "I've been adopted by God. I'm one of His children, and someday I'll spend forever with Him." That's the truest love there is, and it is yours to accept or decline. The love our Father has for us is absolutely life changing: When you become a child of God, you are changed by His grace, changed by His mercy, and changed by His marvelous love! Not a bad way to go through life, huh? So, peace for your journey, and may God's amazing love encompass you.

# ABOUT THE AUTHOR

D r. Jeff Taylor is a pastor, author, public speaker, and counselor living in East Texas. He and his wife Debbie adopted Samantha on June 7th, 2004, and have since aided other couples in the process of adopting daughters from China. The Taylor family resides in the quiet rural East Texas town of Latexo; an area teaming with horses, farm animals, and a slow-paced community that enjoys the simple things in life. Dr. Taylor holds degrees from Hardin-Simmons University, Southwestern Baptist Theological Seminary, and Southern California University. He has worked as a minister for more than 25 years, as well as a nationally certified human resources professional, (SPHR), working for a variety of Fortune 500 companies.

Other books by Dr. Taylor:
*By Their Own Hand: A Survivors' Guide After A Loved One's Suicide*
*Peace, Be Still: Navigating the Storm's of Life*

# END NOTES

1.  Frost, Robert. *The Road Not Taken and Other Poems*. New York: Dover Publications, 1993. Page 1.

2.  Star Wars® is a register trademark of LucasFilm.

3.  *Parenthood*® (1989) is a registered motion picture trademark of Universal Pictures and Imagine Entertainment.

4.  *Somewhere Out There;* written by James Horner, Barry Mann, and Cynthia Weil; from the film An American Tail, (1986). Produced by Amblin Entertainment and Universal Pictures.